Berlitz®

hide
this
spanish
phrase
book

New

Hide This Spanish Phrase Book

Contacting the Editors
Every effort has been made to provide accurate information in this publication, but changes are inevitable. The publisher cannot be responsible for any resulting loss, inconvenience or injury. We would appreciate it if readers would call our attention to any errors or outdated information by contacting Berlitz Publishing, 193 Morris Avenue, Springfield, NJ 07081, USA. email: comments@berlitzbooks.com

First Printing: June 2006
Printed in Canada

Writers: Isabel Mendoza, Maria Amparo Pérez Roch
Editorial Director: Sheryl Olinsky Borg
Senior Editor/Project Manager: Lorraine Sova
Assistant Editor: Emily Bernath
Cover and Interior Design: Wee Design Group, Blair Swick
Production Manager: Elizabeth Gaynor
Illustrations: Kyle Webster, Amy Zaleski

INSIDE

INTRO

So, you're going to a Spanish-speaking country, huh? Well then, you'd better learn a couple of useful phrases. By "useful" we mean the lingo you need to hook up, check in, and hang out. This un-censored phrase book's got you covered with everything you need to speak cool Spanish—saying hi, getting a room, spending your bucks, finding a cheap place to eat, scoring digits... and a helluva lot more. We've even thrown in a few totally offensive, completely inappropriate, and downright nasty terms—just for fun. You'll be able to easily spot these by looking for ▌. Wanna know the best of the worst? Look for ▌.

We've got your back with insider tips, too. Check these out for up-to-date info that'll help you maneuver around a Spanish locale...

FACT   cool facts that may seem like fiction

the scoop   tips on what's hot and what's not

yo!   info you've gotta know

Warning—this language can get you into trouble. If you wanna say it in public, that's up to you. But we're not taking the rap (like responsibility and liability) for any problems you could encounter by using the expressions in Hide This Spanish Phrase Book. These include, but are not limited to, verbal and/or physical abuse, bar brawls, cat fights, arrest... Use caution when dealing with Spanish that's hot!

SPEAK UP

We don't want you to sound like a loser when speaking Spanish. So, to make it easy for you, we've provided really simple phonetics (those are the funky letters right under the Spanish expressions) with every entry you could say out loud. Just read the phonetics as if they're English, e.g.,

What's up? ← *This is English, obviously.*

¿Qué onda? ← *A very cool Spanish expression...*

keh <u>on</u>dah ← *Say this as if it's English. Easy, right?!*

 See this underline? That means you've gotta stress this part of the word.

stress?

If you wanna read the Spanish without checking out the phonetics, remember:

- in words ending with a vowel, -n, or -s, stress the next to last syllable
- in words ending in a consonant, stress the last syllable
- if you see an accent on a letter, that means it's stressed, so put some force behind it!

> **yo!** What's the difference between "el" and "él"? "El" = *the* and "él" = *he*! Words that are spelled the same in Spanish but have different meanings use the accent to differentiate between them.

sex

Meaning gender... Words in Spanish can be masculine or feminine. You'll see ♂ for masculine words and ♀ for the ladies.

Yeah, baby! Now you're ready for some Spanish action.

hi there

Make a good impression on the locals from the get-go.

Hello.

Hola.
<u>o</u>lah
Formal yet friendly.

Good morning!

¡Buenos días!
<u>bweh</u>nos <u>dee</u>ahs
Start your day by greeting the locals with class.

Good afternoon.

Buenas tardes.
<u>bweh</u>nahs <u>tahr</u>dehs
Use this after 12 p.m.

Good evening.

Buenas noches.
<u>bweh</u>nahs <u>no</u>chehs
A formal greeting used after 7 p.m.

How're you doing?

¿Cómo andas?
<u>ko</u>mo <u>ahn</u>dahs
Very casual—very cool.

What's going on?

¡Quiubo!
<u>keew</u>bo
The short form of "¿Qué hubo?"

What's up?

¿Qué onda? MEXICO
keh <u>on</u>dah
Sounds cool everywhere.

How's it going?

¿Cómo van las cosas?
<u>ko</u>mo bahn lahs <u>ko</u>sahs
Very laid-back and relaxed.

the SCOOP

When meeting someone for the first time, knowing the right body language is just as important as saying the right phrases. It's very unusual for young Latinos to shake hands when greeting or being introduced. They prefer to gently hit fists. Sometimes, a friendly glance or a slight nod is enough. Kissing on the cheek (on both cheeks for Spaniards) is also very common, but never between guys, with the exception of Argéntineans, Chileans, and Uruguayans.

what's up

Mix and match these conversation starters.

Questions. . .

How are things?	**¿Qué tal?** *keh tahl*
Hi! How are you?	**¡Hola! ¿Cómo está?** *olah komo ehstah*
How's life?	**¿Qué más de tu vida?** *keh mahs deh too beedah*

Answers. . .

Great!	**¡Excelente!** *ehksehlehn-teh*
Fine / Not bad / OK.	**Bien.** *beeyehn*
Terrible!	**¡Terrible!** *tehrreebleh*

hey you!

Wanna get someone's attention? Try these.

Hey!	**¡Oye!** *oyeh* *Literally: Hear!*
Excuse me!	**¡Disculpe!** *deeskoolpeh*
Look!	**¡Mira!** *meerah* *Just add "chica", girl, or "chico", boy, before "mira" to make it more personal.*
Bro! / Sis!	**¡Compadre♂! / ¡Comadre♀!** *kompahdreh / komahdreh* *Make someone feel like part of the family.*
Hey, bro!	**¡Oiga, hermano♂!** *oy-gah ehrmahno* *Another casual way to get someone to notice you.*

3

sorry

Oops…need to apologize?

My bad.

Disculpa.
dees*kool*pah

Sorry!

¡Lo siento!
lo *seeyehn*-toh
Formal and polite.

Excuse me.

Perdona.
pehr*doh*nah
Informal and casual.

huh?

What did he or she just say? Make sure you understood it correctly!

Excuse me?

¿Perdón? / ¿Cómo? SPAIN
pehr*don* / *komo*

Could you repeat that?

¿Podría repetírmelo?
po*dree*-ah rehpeh*teer*-mehlo

Could you spell it?

¿Podría deletreármelo?
po*dree*-ah dehlehtreh-*ahr*mehlo

Please write it down.

Escríbalo, por favor.
ehs*kree*-bahlo por fah*bor*

Can you translate this
for me?

¿Puede traducirme esto?
*pweh*deh trahdoo-*seer*meh *ehs*to

What does this / that mean?

¿Qué significa esto / eso?
keh seeg-nee-*fee*kah *ehs*to / *ehs*o

Do you speak English?	**¿Habla usted inglés?** _ahblah oostehd eenglehs_ _In case you couldn't understand_ _a word he or she just said, it's_ _OK to ask if he or she speaks_ _your language._
I don't speak (much) Spanish.	**No hablo (mucho) español.** _no ahblo (moocho) ehspanyol_
I don't understand.	**No entiendo.** _no ehnteeyehn-doh_
Do you understand?	**¿Entiende? / ¿Comprende?** _ehnteeyehn-deh / komprehndeh_
Where can I find a translator?	**¿Dónde puedo encontrar a un traductor?** _dondeh pwehdo ehnkontrahr ah oon trahdooktor_ _For those untranslatable or serious_ _situations, you may need this._

help

Got yourself into a sticky situation?

Can you help me?	**¿Puede ayudarme?** _pwehdeh ahyoo-dahrmeh_
Help!	**¡Socorro!** _sokorro_
Go away!	**¡Váyase!** _bahyahseh_
Call the police!	**¡Llamen a la policía!** _yahmehn ah lah polee-seeah_

Fire!	**¡Incendio!**
	een<u>sehn</u>-deeyo
I'm lost.	**Estoy perdido♂ / perdida♀.**
	ehs<u>toy</u> pehr<u>dee</u>do / pehr<u>dee</u>dah
I'm sick.	**Estoy enfermo♂ / enferma♀.**
	ehs<u>toy</u> ehn<u>fehr</u>mo / ehn<u>fehr</u>mah
Get a doctor!	**¡Traigan un doctor!**
	<u>trayee</u>-gahn oon dok<u>tor</u>

emergency

Just in case you get into trouble…

Where's the police station?	**¿Dónde está la estación de policía?**
	<u>don</u>deh ehs<u>tah</u> lah ehstah-<u>seeyon</u> deh polee<u>seeah</u>
I want to report …	**Quiero denunciar …**
	<u>keeyeh</u>-ro dehnoon-<u>seeyahr</u>
an accident.	**un accidente.**
	oon ahksee<u>den</u>teh
a mugging.	**un asalto.**
	oon ah<u>sahl</u>to
a rape.	**una violación.**
	<u>oo</u>nah beeyolah-<u>seeyon</u>
a theft.	**un robo.**
	oon <u>ro</u>bo
I need to contact the consulate.	**Necesito comunicarme con el consulado.**
	nehseh<u>see</u>to komoonee<u>kahr</u>-meh kon ehl konsoo<u>lah</u>do

bye-bye

From classic to cool, here are the best ways to say good-bye.

Good-bye.

Adiós.
ahdeeyos
Always appropriate.

Bye.

Chao.
cha-oh
The standard, but still the coolest
way to say good-bye.

See you later.

Hasta luego.
ahstah lwehgo
A classic.

See you a little later.

Hasta lueguito.
ahstah lweh-geetoh
"Lueguito" is the diminutive of
"luego". Latinos use diminutives
to sound friendly and cute.

I'm out of here.

Me piro.
meh peero
Get right to the point!

See you.

Ahí nos vemos.
ahee nos behmos
It's catchy and cute.

2 GETTIN' AROUND

by plane

Just arrived? Going somewhere? Act like you know what you're doing.

To …, please.	**A …, por favor.**
	ah… por fah<u>bor</u>
	Hint: Top spots include Barcelona,
	Spain; Buenos Aires, Argentina;
	Cancun, Mexico; just to name a few.
One-way. / Round-trip.	**De ida. / De ida y vuelta.**
	deh <u>ee</u>dah / deh <u>ee</u>dah ee <u>bweh</u>ltah
How much?	**¿Cuánto?**
	<u>kwahn</u>to
Are there any discounts?	**¿Hay algún descuento?**
	eye ahl<u>goon</u> dehs<u>kwehn</u>to
	Doesn't hurt to ask!
When is the … flight to …?	**¿A qué hora sale el … vuelo a …?**
	a keh <u>orah</u> <u>sah</u>leh ehl … <u>bweh</u>lo ah
first	**primer**
	pree<u>mehr</u>
next	**próximo**
	<u>prok</u>seemo
last	**último**
	<u>ool</u>teemo
I'd like … ticket(s).	**Quiero … boleto(s) / billete(s).** SPAIN
	<u>keeyeh</u>-ro … bo<u>leh</u>to(s) / bee<u>yeh</u>teh(s)
	Traveling alone or with a "friend"?
one	**un**
	oon
two	**dos**
	dos

9

Is flight … delayed?	**¿Está retrasado el vuelo …?**
	ehstah rehtrah-sahdo ehl bwehlo
	Keep your fingers crossed that it's not!
How late will it be?	**¿Cuánto se demora en llegar?**
	kwahnto seh dehmorah ehn yehgahr
Which gate does flight … leave from?	**¿De qué puerta sale el vuelo …?**
	deh keh pwehrtah sahleh ehl bwehlo
Where is (are) …?	**¿Dónde está(n) …?**
	dondeh ehstah(n)
the baggage check	**el depósito de equipaje**
	ehl dehpo-seeto deh ehkeepah-kheh
the lockers	**los casilleros**
	los kahseeyehros
the luggage carts	**los carritos de equipaje**
	los kahrreetos deh ehkeepah-kheh

Need cheap airline tickets? Do your research online. It's not only sites like cheaptickets.com, expedia.com, orbitz.com that offer great fares and package deals; you should also check out airline sites for special promotions. If that seems like too much work, it doesn't hurt to have someone do the work for you—call a travel agent for help. An agent usually won't charge a fee for research.

in flight

Sit back (if possible) and enjoy.

Can I have an extra blanket / pillow?	**¿Me puede traer una manta / almohada adicional?** *meh pwehdeh trahehr oonah mahntah / ahlmoah-dah ahdeeseeeyo-nahl*
I ordered a … meal.	**Pedí una comida …** *pehdee oonah komeedah*
diabetic	**para diabéticos.** *pahrah deeahbeh-teekos*
gluten-free	**sin gluten.** *seen glootehn*
kosher	**kosher.** *kosehr*
low-calorie / -cholesterol / -fat / -sodium	**baja en calorías / colesterol / grasa / sodio.** *bahkhah ehn kahloree-ahs / kolehsteh-rol / grahsah / sodeeyo*
vegan	**vegan.** *behgahn*
vegetarian	**vegetariana.** *behkhehtah-reeyahnah*
I need a barf bag.	**Necesito una bolsa para vómitos.** *nehseh-seeto oonah bolsah pahrah bomeetos* *Gross.*

11

What does that sign say?

SALIDAS
DEPARTURES

LLEGADAS
ARRIVALS

SEGURIDAD
SECURITY CHECK

NO DESCUIDE SU EQUIPAJE
DO NOT LEAVE BAGS UNATTENDED

your stuff

Find it, grab it, and go!

Where is the luggage from flight …?	**¿Dónde está el equipaje del vuelo …?** *dondeh ehstah ehl ehkeepah-keh dehl bwehlo*
My luggage has been stolen.	**Me han robado mi equipaje.** *meh ahn robahdo mee ehkeepah-keh*
My suitcase was damaged.	**Mi maleta se dañó.** *mee mahlehtah seh dahnyo*
Our luggage hasn't arrived.	**Nuestro equipaje no ha llegado.** *nwehstro ehkeepah-keh no ah yehgahdo* *What a nightmare.*

12

the scoop

Say good-bye to long check-in lines! Some airlines are now offering online check-in. Simply visit the participating airline's website up to 24 hours in advance of your flight and fill in the necessary info. A number of airlines also have airport kiosks available; use one to process your check-in electronically—it'll save you time and hassle. You usually have to check-in at least an hour before take-off. Visit your airline's website for details.

by train

OK, first, you gotta get there.

| How do I get to the train station? | **¿Cómo llego a la estación de tren?**
 komo yehgo ah lah ehstah-seeyon deh trehn |
| How far is it? | **¿A qué distancia está?**
 ah keh deestahn-seeyah ehstah |

waitin' for the train

Learn to negotiate your way around the station.

| Where is (are) the ...? | **¿Dónde está(n) ...?**
 dondeh estah(n) |
| baggage check | **el depósito de equipajes**
 ehl dehpo-seeto deh ehkeepah-khehs |

Where is (are) the …?	**¿Dónde está(n) …?** *dondeh estah(n)*
bathrooms	**los baños** *los bahnyos*
currency exchange	**la oficina de cambio** *lah ofee-seenah deh kahm-beeyo*
information desk	**la oficina de información** *lah ofee-seenah deh eenformah-seeyon*
lockers	**los casilleros** *los kahseeyehros*
lost and found	**la oficina de objetos perdidos** *lah ofee-seenah deh obkhehtos pehrdeedos*
pay phones	**las cabinas telefónicas** *lahs kahbeenahs tehlehfonee-kahs*
platforms	**los andenes** *los ahndehnehs*
snack bar	**la cafetería** *la kahfehteh-reeah*
ticket office	**la venta de boletos** *lah behntah deh bolehtos*
waiting room	**la sala de espera** *lah sahlah deh ehspeh-rah*
I'd like a … ticket to …	**Quisiera un boleto … para …** *keeseeyeh-rah oon bolehto … pahrah*
one-way	**de ida** *deh eedah*
round-trip	**de ida y vuelta** *deh eedah ee bwehl-tah*

How much is that?	**¿Cuánto es?** _kwahnto ehs_
Is there a discount for students?	**¿Hay descuentos para estudiantes?** _eye dehskwehn-tos pahrah ehstoo-deeyahntehs_ _You could save big bucks!_
Do you offer a cheap same-day round-trip fare?	**¿Hay una tarifa especial para viajes de ida y vuelta el mismo día?** _eye oonah tahreefah ehspeh-seeyahl pahrah beeyahkhehs deh eedah ee bwehl-tah ehl meesmo deeah_
Is it cheaper to travel after a certain time?	**¿Sale más barato viajar después de determinada hora?** _sahleh mahs bahrahto beeyah-khahr dehspwehs deh dehtehrmee-nahdah orah_
Could I have a schedule?	**¿Podría darme un horario de trenes?** _podree-ah dahrmeh oon orahreeyo deh trehnehs_
When is the train to …?	**¿A qué hora sale el tren para …?** _ah keh orah sahleh ehl trehn pahrah_
How long is the trip?	**¿Cuánto dura el viaje?** _kwanhto doorah ehl beeyahkheh_ _Prepare yourself._

train talk

Whether you're waiting for the train or looking for a seat, make conversation with a good-looking Latino or Latina.

Hello! Where is platform …?	**¡Hola! ¿Dónde está el andén …?** _olah dondeh ehstah ehl ahndehn_

15

Is this the train to …?	**¿Es éste el tren a …?**
	ehs ehsteh ehl trehn ah
	I bet you're hoping he/she will be on your train.
Hello, hottie. Is this seat taken?	**Hola mamita ♀ / papito ♂.** **¿Está ocupado este asiento?**
	olah mahmeetah / pahpeeto ehstah okoo-pahdo ehsteh ahseeyehn-toh
	Literally "mamita" is mommy and "papito" is daddy.
Hello, baby. Do you mind if I sit here?	**Hola nena ♀. ¿Te molesta si me siento aquí?**
	olah nehnah teh molehstah see meh seeyehn-toh ahkee
	Guys, flirt with the girls a little.

yo! What does that sign say?

RESERVACIONES
RESERVATIONS

INFORMACIÓN
INFORMATION

A LOS ANDENES
TO THE PLATFORMS

SALIDA
EXIT

by bus

It's cheap, so if you are too, this is the way to go.

Where is the bus station?
¿Dónde queda la estación de autobuses?
dondeh kehdah lah ehstah-seeyon deh awtoboo-sehs

Where can I buy tickets?
¿Dónde se compran los boletos?
dondeh seh komprahn los bolehtos

How much is the fare to …?
¿Cuál es la tarifa para …?
kwahl ehs lah tahreefah pahrah

A … ticket to …, please.
Un boleto … para …, por favor.
oon bolehto … pahrah … por fahbor

one-way
de ida
deh eedah

round-trip
de ida y vuelta
deh eedah ee bwehl-tah

Is this the right bus to …?
¿Es éste el autobús para …?
ehs ehsteh ehl awtoboos pahrah

Could you tell me when to get off?
¿Podría decirme cuándo tengo que bajar?
podree-ah dehseermeh kwahndo tehngo keh bahkhar
Just in case you have no clue as to where you're headed…

Next stop, please!
¡La próxima parada, por favor!
lah prokseemah pahrahdah por fahbor
If you want the driver to stop, better say please!

the
SCOOP

Gotta take the bus? There's a bus station—"Central de Autobuses" or "Central Camionera"—in just about every city. The bus itself has a different name, depending on the city you're in: "el bus/autobús" (the general term), "el camión" (Mexico), "el ómnibus" (Peru), "el micro" (Chile), and "la guagua" (Caribbean). If you're going far, try a long-distance bus; they're readily available in Argentina, Chile, and Mexico. Travel first, second, or third class; go "sin escalas" (nonstop), "directo" (few stops), or "ordinario" (on-demand stops).

by subway

Is goin' underground your style? Then you'll need these.

Where's the nearest subway station?	**¿Dónde queda la estación de metro más cercana?** *dondeh kehdah lah ehstah-seeyon deh mehtro mahs sehrkahnah* *Please let it be in walking distance.*
Where do I buy tickets?	**¿Dónde se compran los boletos?** *dondeh seh komprahn los bolehtos*
Could I have a subway map, please?	**¿Me podría dar un mapa del metro, por favor?** *meh podree-ah dahr oon mahpah del mehtro por fahbor*
Which line should I take for ...?	**¿Qué línea debo tomar para ir a ...?** *keh leenehah dehbo tomahr pahrah eer ah* *Ask a cutie for help.*

Which stop is this?	**¿Qué parada es ésta?** *keh pahrahdah ehs ehstah*
Is the next stop …?	**¿Es … la próxima parada?** *ehs … lah prokseemah pahrahdah*
Where are we?	**¿Dónde estamos?** *dondeh ehstahmos* *Don't have a clue, huh?!*

 If you prefer life underground, you'll be able to get a subway ride in Mexico City, Buenos Aires, Santiago, or Caracas. Buy a single flat-rate ticket or a book of tickets, "un abono", at ticket offices or automatic machines, found in every station. The Mexico City "metro" runs from 5–12 a.m. (7–12 a.m. on Sundays) but try to avoid it during rush hour; you can carry only one package, and it can be no bigger than a briefcase!

by taxi

Feelin' lazy? Get a cab.

Where can I get a taxi?	**¿Dónde puedo tomar un taxi?** *dondeh pwehdo tomahr oon tahksee*
Please take me to …	**Por favor, lléveme a …** *por fahbor yehbehmeh ah*
a good bar.	**un buen bar.** *oon bwehn bahr*
a good dance club.	**una buena discoteca.** *oonah bwehnah deesko-tehkah*

19

Please take me to …	**Por favor, lléveme a …** *por fahbor, yehbehmeh ah*
a good club.	**un buen boliche.** ARGENTINA *oon bwehn boleecheh* *Literally: a good bowling alley*
the airport.	**el aeropuerto.** *ehl ahehro-pwehrto*
the train station.	**la estación de tren.** *lah ehstah-seeyon deh trehn*
this address.	**esta dirección.** *ehstah deerehk-seeyon*
How much will it cost?	**¿Cuánto va a costar el viaje?** *kwahnto bah ah kostahr ehl beeyahkheh* *Know before you go.*
How much is that?	**¿Cuánto es?** *kwahnto ehs*
Keep the change.	**Guarde el cambio.** *gwahrdeh ehl kahmbeeyo*

FACT

It's easiest to get a taxi at official taxi stands, found in most major cities, airports, and train and bus terminals. When you grab a cab be sure to ask the fare straight off the bat. Also find out if you have to pay extra for baggage or for night trips—you probably will. Unless your cabbie rocks, you don't have to tip in most Central and South American countries; it's optional in Argentina.

by car

Can't give up the luxury of having your own car?

I'd like to rent …   **Quisiera alquilar …**
                            keeseeyeh-rah ahlkeelahr

an automatic.   **un carro automático.**
                           oon kahrro awtomah-teeko

a car with air conditioning. **un carro con aire acondicionado.**
                             *oon kahrro kon eyereh
                             ahkondeeseeyo-nahdo*

How much does it cost   **¿Cuál es el precio por día /
per day / week?   semana?**
                           *kwahl ehs ehl prehseeyo por deeah /
                           sehmahnah*

Is mileage / insurance   **¿Está incluido el kilometraje /
included?   el seguro?**
                           *ehstah eenklooeedo ehl
                           keelomeh-trahkheh / ehl sehgooro*
                           This can really add up…

Where's the gas station?   **¿Dónde está la gasolinera?**
                           dondeh ehstah lah gahsolee-nehrah

Fill it up, please.   **Llene el tanque, por favor.**
                           yehneh ehl tahnkeh por fahbor

car trouble

Having a breakdown?

My car broke down.   **Mi carro se ha descompuesto.**
                           mee kahrro seh ah dehskom-pwehsto

Can you send a mechanic / tow truck?	**¿Puede enviar un mecánico / una grúa?**
	pwehdeh ehnbeeahr oon mehkahneeko / oonah grooah
I've run out of gas.	**Se me acabó la gasolina.**
	seh meh ahkahbo lah gahsoleenah
	Duh!
I have a flat.	**Tengo una llanta pinchada.**
	tehngo oonah yahntah peenchahdah
I've locked the keys in the car.	**Dejé las llaves dentro del carro.**
	dehkheh lahs yahbehs dehntro dehl kahrro
	Nice one.

Ready for a road trip? Though most Latin American countries don't require it, you should invest in an international driver's license unless you can confirm that your foreign license is valid in the country you're visiting. You'd better get some insurance; it's often available from agencies at the border. Keep your eye out for speed limit signs, posted on all roads—last thing you need is to get pulled over by the police. In case you do, here's some useful lingo:

I had the right of way.	**Yo tenía preferencia.**
	yo tehneeah prehfeh-rehnseeyah
I didn't see the sign.	**Yo no vi la señal.**
	yo noh bee lah sehnyahl
	Excuses, excuses.
I'm a tourist!	**¡Soy turista!**
	soy tooreestah
He ran into me.	**Él me chocó.**
	ehl meh choko

by bike

Calling all bikers...

I'd like to rent a bike.
Quisiera alquilar una bicicleta.
keeseeyeh-rah ahlkee-lahr oonah beesee-klehtah

I'd like to rent ...
Quisiera alquilar ...
keeseeyeh-rah ahlkee-lahr

a moped.
un velomotor.
oon behlomotor

a motorbike.
una motocicleta.
oonah motosee-klehtah

How much does it cost per day / week?
¿Cuál es el precio por día / semana?
kwahl ehs ehl prehseeyo por deeah / sehmahnah
Don't get screwed; confirm the price in advance.

by thumb

Hitchhiking is NOT recommended.

Where are you heading?
¿Adónde va usted?
ahdondeh bah oostehd

Is that on the way to ...?
¿Está eso en la vía a ...?
ehstah ehso ehn lah beeah ah

Could you drop me off here / at ...?
¿Podría dejarme aquí / en ...?
podree-ah dehkhahr-meh ahkee / ehn

Thanks for the ride.
Gracias por el el viaje.
grah-seeyahs por ehl beeyahkheh
It doesn't hurt to be nice.

3 MONEY

get cash

Get your pesos (Argentina, Chile, Colombia, Mexico), bolívares (Venezuela), or euros (Spain) and start spending your money!

Where's the nearest …?	**¿Dónde está … más cercano♂ / cercana♀?** *dondeh ehstah … mahs sehrkahno / sehrkahnah*
ATM	**el cajero automático** *ehl kahkhero awtomah-teeko* *Shorten it to just "el cajero".*
bank	**el banco** *ehl bahnko*
currency exchange office	**la oficina de cambio** *lah ofeesee-nah deh kahmbeeyo*
Can I exchange foreign currency here?	**¿Puedo cambiar moneda extranjera aquí?** *pwehdo kahm-beeyahr monehdah ehkstrahn-khehrah ahkee*
I'd like to change some dollars / pounds into pesos / euros.	**Quisiera cambiar dólares / libras esterlinas a pesos / euros.** *keeseeyeh-rah kahm-beeyahr dolahrehs / leebrahs ehstehrleenahs ah pehsos / eh-ooros*
I want to cash some travelers checks.	**Quisiera cambiar unos cheques de viajero.** *keeseeyeh-rah kahm-beeyahr oonos chehkehs deh beeyah-khehro*

What's the exchange rate? **¿Cuál es la tasa de cambio?**
kwahl ehs lah tahsah deh kahmbeeyo
If you're concerned about the changing rates, charge it—you'll get that day's rate as calculated by your credit card company.

How much commission do
you charge?
¿Cuánto es la comisión?
kwahnto ehs lah komee-seeyon
Watch out for those hidden fees.

 Get the best rate for your dollars or pounds by exchanging your money at "oficina / casa de cambio", a currency exchange office. They can be found in most tourist centers and often offer better exchange rates than hotels and banks. Keep in mind that you've gotta bring your passport when you wanna change money!

ATM

Get cash fast.

Where are the ATMs
[cash machines]?
¿Dónde están los cajeros automáticos?
dondeh ehstahn los kahkhehros awtomah-teekos

Can I use my …
card in the ATM?
¿Puedo usar mi tarjeta … en este cajero automático?
pwehdo oosahr mee tahrkhehtah … ehn ehsteh kahkhehro awtomah-teeko

The ATM has eaten my
card.
El cajero automático se ha quedado con mi tarjeta.
ehl kahkhehro awtomah-teeko seh ah kehdahdo kon mee tahrkhehtah
Good luck getting another one!

FACT Get cash 24-7 just about anywhere in Latin America. If you have an ATM, bank, or credit card you should be able to withdraw money from most ATMs or bank machines in cities and larger towns in Latin America. If your PIN number is a word, make sure you memorize the number equivalents since many foreign ATMs don't have letters on their key pads. You'll probably get hit with some stiff fees by both your bank and the card's network (e.g., Cirrus, Explore, Interlink, Plus, Star, etc.) for accessing the International ATM System. Call your bank in advance to find out its international ATM withdrawal fees.

charge it

Can't figure out the currency exchange? Avoid the hassle and use your credit card.

Can I withdraw money on my credit card here?	**¿Puedo retirar dinero con mi tarjeta de crédito aquí?** *pwehdo rehteerahr deenehro kon mee tahrkhehtah deh krehdeeto ahkee*
Can I pay by credit card?	**¿Puedo pagar con tarjeta de crédito?** *pwehdo pahgahr kon tahrkhehtah deh krehdeeto*
I'll pay by credit card.	**Voy a pagar con tarjeta de crédito.** *boy ah pahgahr kon tahrkhehtah deh krehdeeto*

FACT You may be charged an international transaction fee—for each purchase you make abroad—if you use a bank-issued credit card. Contact the credit card provider for more info.

pay up

Here's how to part with your hard-earned dough.

Where do I pay?
¿Dónde se paga?
donsdeh seh pahgah

How much is that?
¿Cuánto cuesta eso?
kwahnto kwehstah ehso
You can also simply say,
¿Cuánto cuesta?

Is it on sale?
¿Tiene descuento?
teeyeh-neh dehskwehnto

Do you accept travelers checks?
¿Aceptan cheques de viajero?
ahsehptahn chehkehs deh beeyah-khehro

I'll pay in cash.
Voy a pagar en efectivo.
boy ah pahgahr ehn ehfehkteebo

Sorry, I don't have enough money.
Disculpe, no tengo suficiente dinero.
deeskoolpeh no tehngo soofee-seeyehnteh deenehro
How embarrassing.

Could I have a receipt, please?
¿Me podría dar un recibo, por favor?
meh podree-ah dahr oon rehseebo por fahbor

HOTEL

get a room

You know you want to.

Can you recommend a hotel in …?
¿Puede recomendarme un hotel en …?
pwehdeh rehkomehndahr-meh oon otehl ehn
You may want to end that question with Oaxaca (Mexico), Buenos Aires (Argentina), Cusco (Peru); they're some of the trendiest destinations in Latin America.

Is it near the center of town?
¿Está cerca del centro?
ehstah sehrkah dehl sehntro
You've gotta be close to where the bars and clubs are, right?

How much is it per night?
¿Cuánto cuesta por noche?
kwahnto kwehstah por nocheh

Is there anything cheaper?
¿Hay algo más barato?
eye ahlgo mahs bahrahto

I have a reservation.
Tengo una reservación.
tehngo oonah rehsehrbah-seeyon

My name is …
Me llamo …
meh yahmo

I confirmed by e-mail.
Confirmé por correo electrónico.
konfeermeh por korreho ehlehk-troneeko

Here's my confirmation number.
Éste es mi número de confirmación.
ehsteh ehs mee noomehro deh konfeermah-seeyon

at the hotel

Need a room for tonight? Ask the right questions.

Do you have a room? **¿Tiene habitaciones disponibles?**
teeyeh-neh ahbeetah-seeyonehs deesponee-blehs

I'd like a single / double room. **Quisiera una habitación sencilla / doble.**
keeseeyeh-rah oonah ahbeetah-seeyon sehnseeyah / dobleh

I'd like a room with a double bed / twin beds. **Quisiera una habitación con cama doble / dos camas.**
keeseeyeh-rah oonah ahbeetah-seeyon kon kahmah dobleh / dos kahmahs
Get a double if you want to snuggle with someone; two twin beds if you're sick and tired of the person you're traveling with.

I'd like a room with a bath / shower. **Quisiera una habitación con baño / ducha.**
keeseeyeh-rah oonah ahbeetah-seeyon kon bahnyo / doochah
It'll cost ya…

gotta have

Things you can't do without.

Is there (a) … in the room? **¿Hay … en la habitación?**
eye … ehn lah ahbeetah-seeyon

air conditioning **aire acondicionado**
ayreh ahkondeeseeyo-nahdo

phone **teléfono**
tehlehfono

TV **televisor**
tehlehbeeso

31

Does the hotel have (a) …?	**¿El hotel tiene …?**
	ehl otehl teeyeh-neh
Wi-Fi® area	**conexión inalámbrica a internet**
	konehk-seeyon eenahlahm-breekah
	ah eentehrneht
internet access	**acceso a internet**
	ahksehso ah eentehrneht
swimming pool	**piscina**
	pees-seenah
restaurant	**restaurante**
	restawrahn-teh
room service	**servicio de habitación**
	sehrbee-seeyo deh ahbeetah-seeyon

price

It all comes down to one thing.

How much is it per night / week?	**¿Cuánto cuesta la noche / la semana?**
	kwahnto kwehstah lah nocheh / lah sehmahnah
Does the price include breakfast?	**¿El precio incluye el desayuno?**
	ehl prehseeyo eenklooyeh ehl dehsahyoono
Do I have to leave a deposit?	**¿Tengo que dejar un depósito?**
	tehngo keh dehkhahr oon dehposeeto
I'd like to speak to the manager.	**Quisiera hablar con el gerente.**
	keeseeyeh-rah ahblahr kon ehl khehrehnteh
	Wanna negotiate a better price?

problems

Tell 'em what's bothering you.

I've lost my key.	**Perdí la llave.** *perhdee lah yahbeh*
I've locked myself out of my room.	**Me he quedado fuera de la habitación.** *meh eh kehdahdo fwehrah deh lah ahbeetah-seeyon*
The lock is broken.	**La cerradura está rota.** *lah sehrrahdoorah ehstah rotah* *Seems a bit dangerous...*
The ... doesn't work.	**... no funciona.** *no foonseeyo-nah*
air conditioning	**El aire acondicionado** *ehl ayeereh ahkondeeseeyo-nahdo*
fan	**El ventilador** *ehl behnteelahdor*
heat	**La calefacción** *lah kahlehfahk-seeyon*
light	**La luz** *lah loos*
I can't turn the heat on / off.	**No puedo encender / apagar la calefacción.** *no pwehdo ehnsehndehr / ahpahgahr lah kahlehfahk-seeyon*
There is no hot water / toilet paper.	**No hay agua caliente / papel higiénico.** *no eye ahgwah kahleeyehn-teh / pahpehl eekheeyeh-neeko*

FACT

Don't get burnt out. If you bring your own electrical gizmos to Latin America, you may need to buy an adapter to fit the various types of electrical sockets. The 110-volt, 60-cycle AC is the norm throughout Central America, Colombia, Mexico, and Venezuela. Further south, the 220-volt, 50-cycle operates in Argentina, Bolivia (except La Paz), Chile, Paraguay, Peru, and Uruguay.

necessities

More importantly…

Where's the bar?

¿Dónde está el bar?
dondeh ehstah ehl bahr
This may be the most important expression in the entire book.

Where's the swimming pool?

¿Dónde está la piscina?
dondeh ehstah lah pee-seenah

Where are the bathrooms?

¿Dónde están los baños?
dondeh ehstahn los bahnyos

What time is the front door locked?

¿A qué hora se cierra la puerta principal?
a keh orah seh seeyeh-rrah lah pwehrtah preenseepahl
If you're staying at a guest house, bed and breakfast, or even a hostel, you may have a curfew!

What time is breakfast served?	**¿A qué hora se sirve el desayuno?** *ah keh orah seh seerbeh ehl dehsahyoono*
Could you wake me at …?	**¿Podría despertarme a las …?** *podree-ah dehspehr-tahrmeh ah lahs*
Can I leave this in the safe?	**¿Puedo dejar esto en la caja de seguridad?** *pwehdo dehkhahr ehsto ehn lah kahkhah deh sehgoo-reedahd*
May I have an extra …?	**¿Me puede traer … adicional?** *meh pwehdeh trahehr … ahdeeseeyo-nahl*

towel	**una toalla** *oonah toahyah*
blanket	**una manta** *oonah mahntah*
pillow	**una almohada** *oonah ahlmoahdah*
roll of toilet paper	**un rollo de papel higiénico** *oon royo deh pahpehl eekheeyeh-neeko*

Are there any messages for me?	**¿Hay algún recado para mí?** *eye ahlgoon rehkahdo pahrah mee* *Waiting for that special someone to call?*

hostel

Looking for budget accommodations? The language you need is right here.

Do you have any places left for tonight?	**¿Tiene cupo disponible para esta noche?** *teeyeh-neh koopo deesponeebleh pahrah ehstah nocheh*

| Do you rent out bedding? | **¿Alquila usted la ropa de cama?** |
| | *ahlkeelah oostehd lah ropah deh kahmah* |

| What time are the doors locked? | **¿A qué hora se cierran las puertas?** |
| | *a keh orah seh seeyeh-rrahn lahs pwehrtahs* |

I have an International Student Card.	**Tengo credencial internacional de estudiante.**
	tehngo krehdehn-seeyahl eentehrnah-seeyonahl deh ehstoodeeyahn-teh
	You may need one in order to stay at certain hostels.

the scoop

Hostels are a great way to get to know young travelers from Latin America and elsewhere. Argentina has almost 50 hostels country-wide, Costa Rica has more than 15, Chile and Mexico each have a dozen or so. If dormitory-style accommodations aren't for you, try booking in advance, online, or by phone. Though many hostels offer single and/or double rooms, they're usually reserved weeks ahead of time by savvy travelers who enjoy their privacy. Visit www.hiusa.org for more info.

check out

It's time to go.

| What time do we have to check out? | **¿A qué hora debemos desocupar la habitación?** |
| | *ah keh orah dehbehmos dehsokoopahr la ahbeetah-seeyon* |

| The bill, please. | **La cuenta, por favor.** |
| | *lah kwehntah por fahbor* |

| Could I have a receipt? | **¿Me podría dar un recibo?** |
| | *meh podree-ah dahr oon rehseebo* |

Do you take credit cards?	**¿Acepta tarjetas de crédito?**
	ahsehptah tahrkhehtahs deh krehdeeto
	Cross your fingers that they do.

I think there's a mistake in this bill.	**Creo que hay un error en esta cuenta.**
	kreho keh eye oon ehrror ehn ehstah kwehntah
	Oh, really?

| I've made ... telephone calls. | **Hice ... llamadas.** |
| | *eeseh ... yahmahdahs* |

I've taken ... from the mini-bar.	**Tomé ... del mini-bar.**
	tomeh ... dehl meenee-bahr
	You lush.

camping

If camp is your thing, here's the info you need.

| Is there a campsite nearby? | **¿Hay alguna zona de campamento por aquí?** |
| | *eye ahlgoo-nah sonah deh kahmpah-mehnto por ahkee* |

| Do you have space for a tent? | **¿Tiene sitio para una tienda de campaña?** |
| | *teeyeh-neh seeteeyo pahrah oonah teeyehn-dah deh kahmpahnyah* |

37

What is the charge per day / week?	**¿Cuál es el precio por día / por semana?**
	kwahl ehs ehl prehseeyo por deeah / por sehmahnah
Are there cooking facilities on site?	**¿Se puede cocinar en la zona de campamento?**
	seh pwehdeh koseenahr ehn lah sonah deh kahmpah-mehnto
Where are the showers?	**¿Dónde están las duchas?**
	dondeh ehstahn lahs doochahs
	Nature sure is dirty, isn't it?!

FACT

Think that campgrounds are for hippies only? Camping is really popular in Mexico and parts of South America. Because of the many campers out there, try to get a permit in advance. In Argentina, most cities have sites where tents can be pitched. Camping and sleeping on the beach is allowed in Mexico but isn't recommended, for safety reasons.

where to eat

What are ya in the mood for?

Let's go to …	**Vamos a …**
	bahmos ah
a restaurant.	**un restaurante.**
	oon rehstawrahn-teh
a bar.	**un bar.**
	oon bahr
a café.	**un café.**
	oon kahfeh
a pastry shop.	**una pastelería.**
	oonah pahstehleh-reeah
an ice-cream parlor.	**una heladería.**
	oonah ehlahdeh-reeah
the snack bar.	**el quiosco de golosinas.**
	ehl keeosko deh goloseenahs

yo!   Want some food? Ask for it the way the locals do.

la comida
lah komeedah

la jama COSTA RICA, CUBA, ECUADOR, PERU, PUERTO RICO
lah khahmah

el morfi ARGENTINA
ehl morfee

el papeo SPAIN
ehl pahpeho

yo!

Now that you know where to eat, you'd better learn *when* to eat.

el desayuno
ehl dehsah<u>yoo</u>no
If you like to sleep in, then Latin America is the place for you. You can have your breakfast from 8–10 a.m.

el almuerzo
ehl ah<u>lmweh</u>rso
Take your time over lunch, just like the locals do; enjoy this meal between 1–4 p.m.

la cena
lah <u>seh</u>nah
Dinner's served after 8 p.m. Get ready for some late nights!

fast food

In a rush? Grab a quick bite to eat so you can keep sightseeing.

I'd like …, please.	**Quiero …, por favor.** *<u>keeyeh</u>-ro … por fah<u>bor</u>*
a burger	**una hamburguesa** *<u>oo</u>nah ahmboor-<u>geh</u>sah*
fries	**papas fritas** *<u>pah</u>pahs <u>free</u>tahs*
a sandwich	**un sandwich** *oon <u>sahn</u>weech*
It's to go.	**Es para llevar.** *ehs <u>pah</u>rah yeh<u>bahr</u>*
That's all, thanks.	**Eso es todo, gracias.** *<u>eh</u>so ehs <u>to</u>do <u>grah</u>-seeyahs*

table manners

Go ahead, treat yourself. You deserve a meal at a swanky restaurant!

A table for two, please.
Una mesa para dos, por favor.
oonah mehsah pahrah dos por fahbor
On a date?

We have a reservation.
Tenemos una reservación.
tehnehmos oonah rehserbah-seeyon
It's always good to think ahead.

Could we sit …?
¿Podemos sentarnos …?
podehmos sehntarnos
Find a cozy, romantic spot.

over there
allá
ahyah

outside
afuera
ahfwehrah

in a non-smoking area
en la sección de no fumadores
ehn lah sehkseeyon deh no foomah-dorehs

by the window
cerca de la ventana
sehrkah deh lah behntahnah

Waiter! / Waitress!
¡Mesero♂! / ¡Mesera♀!
mehsehro / mehsehrah

Could you tell me what … is?
¿Podría explicarme qué es …?
podree-ah eksplee-kahrmeh keh ehs
Avoid the shock when your meal arrives.

What's in it?
¿Qué ingredientes tiene?
keh eengreh-deeyentehs teeyeh-neh

No … please!
¡Sin … por favor!
seen … por fahbor

May I have some …?	**¿Podría traerme un poco de …?**
	podree-ah trahehrmeh oon poko deh
	Check the dictionary in the back to fill in the blank!
May I have …, please?	**¿Podría traerme …, por favor?**
	podree-ah trahehrmeh … por fahbor

a fork	**un tenedor**
	oon tehnehdor
a glass	**un vaso**
	oon bahso
a knife	**un cuchillo**
	oon koocheeyo
a napkin	**una servilleta**
	oonah sehrbeeyehtah
a plate	**un plato**
	oon plahto
a spoon	**una cuchara**
	oonah koochahrah

Where are the bathrooms?	**¿Dónde están los baños?**
	dondeh ehstahn los bahnyos
	Good question.
I can't eat food containing …	**No puedo consumir alimentos que contengan …**
	no pwehdo konsoomeer ahlee-mehntos keh kontengahn
	Allergic to something? Make sure you explain.
Do you have vegetarian meals?	**¿Tiene comida vegetariana?**
	teeyeh-neh komeedah behkhehtah-reeyahnah

watch your mouth

What's the problem?

It's hot.
Está caliente.
ehstah kahleeyehn-teh
Use this to refer to temperature,
not spiciness.

Is it hot?
¿Es picante?
ehs peekahnteh
Spicy hot!

He / She is choking!
¡Está atorado♂ / atorada♀!
ehstah ahtorahdo / ahtorahda
Just in case...

complaints

Go ahead and make a big stink.

That's not what I ordered.
Esto no es lo que yo pedí.
ehsto no ehs lo keh yo pehdee

I asked for …
Yo pedí …
yo pehdee

The food is cold.
La comida está fría.
lah komeedah ehstah freeah

This isn't fresh.
Esto no está fresco.
ehsto no ehstah frehsko

This isn't clean.
Esto no está limpio.
ehsto no ehstah leempeeyo

Don't put up with a nasty waiter.

– ¡Mesero! ¿Cuánto tiempo va a tardar nuestra comida?
meh_seh_ro kwahn_to tee_yehm-po bah ah tahr_dahr nwehs_trah ko_mee_dah
Waiter! How much longer will our food be?

– No lo sé.
no lo seh
I don't know.

– No podemos esperar más.
no po_deh_mos ehspeh_rahr mahs
We can't wait any longer.

good or gross?

Give the chef a compliment—or not.

The meal is …	**La comida está …**
	lah ko_mee_dah ehs_tah
delicious.	**deliciosa.**
	dehlee-seeyosah
exquisite.	**exquisita.**
	ehkskee-seetah
good.	**buena.**
	bwehnah
succulent.	**suculenta.**
	sookoo-lehntah

The meal is …	**La comida está …**
	lah ko__mee__dah eh__stah__
bad.	**mala.**
	__mah__lah
disgusting.	**asquerosa.**
	ahskeh-__ro__sah
horrible.	**horrenda.**
	o__rrehn__dah
so-so.	**regular.**
	rehgoo__lahr__

This is yummy!

> **¡Qué delicia!**
> *keh deh__lee__-seeyah*
> *Literally: What a delight!*
>
> **¡Qué ricura!**
> *keh ree__koo__rah*
> *Literally: What deliciousness!*
>
> **¡Ñami!**
> *__nyah__mee*
> *Literally: Yummy!*

This is yucky!

> **¡Buac!**
> *bwahk*
>
> **¡Guácala!**
> *__wah__kahla*

pay up

How much did that meal set you back?

The check, please.	**La cuenta, por favor.** *lah kwehntah por fahbor*
We'd like to pay separately.	**Queremos pagar por separado.** *kehrehmos pahgahr por sehpahrahdo* *Goin' Dutch?*
It's all together, please.	**Todo junto, por favor.** *todo khoonto por fahbor*
I think there's a mistake in this check.	**Creo que hay un error en esta cuenta.** *kreho keh eye oon ehrror ehn ehstah kwehntah*
I didn't have that. I had …	**Yo no comí eso. Yo comí …** *yo no komee ehso. yo komee*
Is service included?	**¿Está incluido el servicio?** *ehstah eenkloo-eedo ehl sehrbee-seeyo* *Sometimes it is, sometimes it isn't—always best to ask.*
Can I pay with this credit card?	**¿Puedo pagar con esta tarjeta de crédito?** *pwehdo pahgahr kon ehstah tahrkhehtah deh krehdeeto*
I've forgotten my wallet.	**He olvidado mi billetera.** *eh olbeedahdo mee beeyehtehrah* *Ready to wash dishes?!*
I don't have enough money.	**No tengo suficiente dinero.** *no tehngo soofee-seeyenteh deenehro* *Pretty embarrassing…*

47

| Could I have a receipt? | **¿Me podría dar un recibo?** |
| | *meh podreeah dahr oon rehseebo* |

FACT

To tip or not to tip?

Argentina: It's common to tip around 10% in restaurants.

Chile: A service charge isn't included in the bill; it's the norm to leave a 10% tip.

Costa Rica: Most restaurants add a 10% service charge to the bill, so leaving an extra tip isn't expected.

Mexico: Restaurant bills rarely include a service fee, so tip 10–15%.

Puerto Rico: Tip about 15% in restaurants since no service charge is added to the bill.

Venezuela: There's a 10% service charge added to bills but it's customary to leave an extra 5–10% for the wait staff.

Spain: Spaniards never tip unless the service has been extraordinary.

If you're unsure how much to tip, just ask a local:

| How much do you tip? | **¿Cuánto das de propina?** |
| | *kwahnto dahs deh propeenah* |

breakfast

Whether you have it early or late, ask for…

I'll have …	**Tomaré / Quiero …** SPAIN
	tomahreh / keeyeh-ro
coffee.	**café.**
	kahfeh
tea.	**té.**
	teh

butter.	**mantequilla.** _mahntehkee-yah_
eggs.	**huevos.** _wehbos_
fried eggs.	**huevos fritos.** _wehbos freetos_
scrambled eggs.	**huevos revueltos.** _wehbos rehbwehltos_
honey.	**miel.** _meeyehl_
jam.	**mermelada.** _mehrmehlahdah_
juice.	**jugo / zumo.** SPAIN _khoogo / thoomo_
grapefruit juice.	**jugo de toronja.** _khoogo deh toronkhah_
orange juice.	**jugo de naranja.** _khoogo deh nahrahnkha_
milk.	**leche.** _lehcheh_
rolls.	**bollitos.** _boyeetos_
toast.	**pan tostado.** _pahn tostahdo_

¡Ñami!

the SCOOP

Did you wake up with a massive hangover? Go out and order yourself a bowl of "menudo", a traditional Mexican soup that many swear by as an antidote for hangovers. You'll be sober in no time with this spicy, hot, and filling dish—it's made with tripe, hominy, lots of garlic, red chiles, and tons of spices.

yo! In Mexico? You've gotta try the "antojitos mexicanos", authentic Mexican appetizers. Enjoy 'em with a local beer, "Dos Equis" or "Sol", just to name a couple.

guacamole
gwahkah-moleh
mashed avocado, lime juice, and chilies

quesadilla
kehsahdeeyah
"tortilla", a cornmeal pancake, stuffed with cheese and/or other fillings; also served fried and often topped with chili sauce, cream, and more cheese

tostadas
tostahdahs
fried "tortilla" with different fillings

tacos
tahkos
"tortillas" stuffed with all kinds of meat, vegetable, and cheese fillings

tacos dorados
tahkos dorahdos
"tacos" fried in hot oil, spiced with chili-pepper sauce, and served with guacamole, cream, cheese, and lettuce

soup

Homemade and delicious—here are the top picks.

cazuela de mariscos ARGENTINA
kahs.wehlah deh mahreeskos
a flavorful seafood stew

cazuela de ave CHILE
kahs.wehlah deh ahbeh
chicken soup with green vegetables

cocido PERU
koseedo
made with chunks of beef, chicken, or fish, and local vegetables
or roots

chipi-chipi VENEZUELA
cheepee cheepee
clam soup
What a fun word to say! Who wouldn't want to order this?

And the good ol' standards…

bean soup	**sopa de frijoles**
	sopah deh freekholehs
fish soup	**sopa de pescado**
	sopah deh pehskahdo
onion soup	**sopa de cebolla**
	sopah deh sehboyah
rice soup	**sopa de arroz**
	sopah deh ahrros
(green) vegetable soup	**sopa de verduras**
	sopah deh behrdoorahs

fish

The coastal areas of Latin America are well known for their fish and seafood. You've gotta try…

ceviche
sehbeecheh
raw fish, marinated in lemon juice, served with onions and hot peppers

pescado a la veracruzana
pehskahdo ah lah behrahkroo-sahnah
red snapper with tomatoes and pimientos

viudo de pescado
beeoo-doh deh pehskahdo
fish stew, traditionally cooked in holes dug in the ground and covered with hot stones; a favorite of Colombia

Or stick with your favorites…

bass	**mero** *mehro*
cod	**bacalao** *bahkahlaho*
lobster	**langosta** *lahngohstah*
salmon	**salmón** *sahlmon*
shrimp	**gambas / camarones** *gahmbahs / kahmah-ronehs*
sole	**lenguado** *lehngwahdo*

| swordfish | **pez espada** |
| | *pehs ehspahdah* |

| trout | **trucha** |
| | *troochah* |

| tuna | **atún** |
| | *ahtoon* |

you carnivore

If it's meat you want, it's definitely Latin America—specifically Argentina—that you should be visiting. Here are the must haves.

parrillada mixta ARGENTINA
pahrreeyah-dah meekstah
a world-famous mixed grill of different cuts of beef

pollo en mole MEXICO
poyo ehn moleh
chicken in a sauce of chiles, oil, sugar, sesame seeds, peanuts, cocoa, cinnamon, and more, served with small pieces of bread

anticucho PERU
ahnteekoocho
heart (beef) on skewers, broiled over charcoal, and served with hot sauce

Not sure what to order? Stick with the basics.

| bacon | **panceta** |
| | *pahnsehtah* |

| beef | **carne de res** |
| | *kahrneh deh rehs* |

| chicken | **pollo** |
| | *poyo* |

ham	**jamón**
	khahmon
lamb	**cordero**
	kordehro
pork	**cerdo / chancho**
	sehrdo / chahncho
turkey	**pavo**
	pahbo
veal	**ternera**
	tehrnehrah

herbivore

For something a little lighter, try these favorites.

chile
cheeleh
chili peppers or hot peppers—call them what you like; the most popular varieties are: **poblano**, **chipotle**, **jalapeño**, **largo**, **piquín**; but you'll also see **habanero**, **serrano**, and **pimiento**

papas / patatas SPAIN
pahpahs / pahtahtahs
potatoes—the original comfort food; may be ~ **fritas** (fries), ~ **hervidas** (boiled), **puré de** ~ (mashed); and varieties of sweet potatoes: **batatas**, **camotes**, **yame**, and **yuca**

Or sample any of these…

apples	**manzanas**
	mahnsahnahs
beans	**frijoles**
	freekholehs

carrots	**zanahorias** _sahnaho-reeyahs_
corn	**elote / maíx** _ehloteh / mahees_
cucumber	**pepino** _pehpeeno_
eggplant	**berenjena** _behrehn-khehnah_
garlic	**ajo** _ahkho_
lettuce	**lechuga** _lehchoogah_
mushrooms	**champiñones** _chahmpeenyonehs_
onions	**cebollas** _sehboyahs_
oranges	**naranjas** _nahrahnkhahs_
peaches	**duraznos / melocotones** _doorahsnos / mehlokotonehs_
pineapple	**piña** _peenyah_
strawberries	**fresas** _frehsahs_
zucchini	**zapallitos** _sahpahyeetos_

cheese please

Latin America has an amazing selection of local cheese. Try...

asadero
ahsahdehro
a soft, creamy cheese

queso añejo
kehso ahnyehkho
ewe's milk cheese, a little salty

queso de Chihuahua
kehso deh cheewahwah
a popular soft cheese named after a province in Mexico

queso de Oaxaca
kehso deh oahkhakah
very popular in the south of Mexico, used to make "quesadillas"

queso enchilado
kehso ehncheelahdo
same as "queso añejo" but a little sharper in taste; the exterior
is colored with red chili peppers

queso fresco
kehso frehsko
fresh white cheese; made and sold the same day

dessert

End your meal with any one of these delicious sweets.

alborotos
ahlborotos
dessert made of roasted corn

ante
ahnteh
pastry with coconut and almonds

bizcocho
beeskocho
sponge cake

churros
choorros
sticks of fried, sugared dough

cocada
kokahdah
dessert made of coconut

espumilla
ehspoomeeyah
a kind of meringue

flan
flahn
caramel custard / crème caramel

Or simply have…

cookies	**galletas**
	gahyehtahs
cake	**pastel**
	pahstehl
ice cream	**helado**
	ehlahdo
chocolate	**de chocolate**
	deh chkolahteh
strawberry	**de fresa**
	deh frehsah
vanilla	**de vainilla**
	deh bahneeyah

overeating

Did you just pig out?

I'm so full.	**Tengo una llenura.** *tehngo oonah yehnoorah*
I'm about to explode!	**¡Quedé que me exploto!** *kehdeh keh meh ehksploto*
The food didn't agree with me.	**La comida me cayó como una patada.** *lah komeedah meh kahyo komo oonah pahtahdah* *Literally: The food fell on me like a kick.*
No, thanks. I'm on a diet.	**No, gracias. Estoy a dieta.** *no grah-seeyahs ehstoy ah deeyehtah* *A good excuse…*
I feel like …	**Tengo ganas de …** *tehngo gahnahs deh*
throwing up.	**devolver.** *dehbolbehr*
puking.	**trasbocar.** *trahsbokahr* *Literally: bringing up*
vomiting.	**vomitar.** *bomeetahr*

DRINKS

what to drink

When you need to detox, ask for…

I'd like …
Quisiera …
kee<u>seeyeh</u>-rah

coffee.
un café.
oon kah<u>feh</u>

tea.
un té.
oon teh

hot chocolate.
un chocolate caliente.
oon choko<u>lah</u>teh kah<u>leeyehn</u>-teh

mineral water.
un agua mineral.
oon <u>ah</u>gwah meeneh-<u>rahl</u>

carbonated /
non-carbonated
con gas / sin gas
kon gahs / seen gahs

A black coffee / coffee
with milk.
Un café solo / con leche.
oon kah<u>feh</u> <u>solo</u> / kon <u>leh</u>cheh

the scoop

You can get a good cup of coffee just about everywhere in Latin America. Try: "café chico" (thick, dark in small cup); "~ con crema" (with cream); "~ con leche" (with milk); "~ cortado" (with a little milk); "~ descafeinado" (decaffeinated).

If tea's your thing, you're gonna have to visit Argentina, where "yerba mate", an herbal tea, is served in hollowed out gourds and sipped with a special straw. Just because it's herbal doesn't mean that "yerba mate" doesn't have some kick—it's packed with caffeine.

beer

Ready for a buzz?

Do you have … beer? **¿Tienen cerveza …?**
teeyeh-nehn sehrbehsah

   bottled   **en botella**
            ehn botehyah

   draft   **de barril**
            deh bahrreel

yo! Wanna beer? Ask for a cold one like a local.

una cerveza
oonah sehrbehsah

una chela MEXICO
oonah chehlah

una birra CHILE, ECUADOR, BOLIVIA, MEXICO, NICARAGUA, PERU
oonah beerrah

una fría COLOMBIA, GUATEMALA, MEXICO, PANAMA, PUERTO RICO,
oonah freeah VENEZUELA

una pola COLOMBIA
oonah polah

una rubia COSTA RICA, PERU
oonah roobeeyah

una biela ECUADOR
oonah beeyehlah

una birria EL SALVADOR
oonah beerreeyah

the SCOOP

Now that you know how to ask for a beer, here's the next step: Request a local brand.

Escudo *ehs<u>koo</u>do* CHILE

Imperial *eempeh-<u>ree</u>yahl* COSTA RICA

Bohemia, Dos Equis, Pacífico, Sol, Superior, Tecate, Negra Modelo, Tres Equis *bo<u>eh</u>meeyah, dos <u>eh</u>kees, pah<u>see</u>feeko, sol, soopeh<u>ree</u>yor, teh<u>kah</u>teh, <u>neh</u>grah mo<u>deh</u>hlo, trehs <u>eh</u>kees* MEXICO

Cuzqueña *koos<u>keh</u>nyah* PERU

Polar *po<u>lahr</u>* VENEZUELA

shots!

There's no faster way to get a party started.

I'd like a shot of …	**Quiero un trago de …** *<u>keeyeh</u>-ro oon <u>trah</u>go deh*
gin.	**ginebra / gin.** *khee<u>neh</u>-brah / "gin"*
liqueur.	**licor.** *lee<u>kor</u>*
vodka.	**vodka.** *<u>bod</u>kah*
whisky.	**whisky.** *<u>wees</u>kee*

To tip or not to tip?

Argentina: The "propinas", tips, range from 10%–15%; it depends on how many drinks you've had!

Mexico: Tip bartenders—especially in resort areas like Acapulco and Cancun—10%–15% of the bill.

Puerto Rico: Tip about 10% in bars.

Spain: Round up your bill to the nearest euro (€).

the scoop

Wanna know what the locals drink?

tequila
teh<u>kee</u>lah
the famous Mexican spirit, distilled from cactus

mescal
mehs<u>kahl</u>
a less refined version of tequila; the bottle contains "un gusano", a worm, to prove its authenticity

caña
<u>kah</u>nyah
a high proof alcohol made from sugar cane

ron
ron
some of the best rum is produced in Puerto Rico

wino

Go ahead and order a glass—or bottle—of the best.

May I see the wine list? | **¿Puedo ver la lista de vinos?**
pwehdoh behr lah leestah deh beenos
Try a local wine; you'll be impressed.

I'd like … of red / white wine. | **Quisiera … de vino tinto / blanco.**
keeseeyeh-rah … deh beeno teento / blahnko

a bottle | **una botella**
oonah botehyah

a carafe | **una garrafa**
oonah gahrrahfah

a glass | **un vaso**
oon bahso

As you probably already know, it's easy to make friends at a bar…

– ¿Quieres tomar algo?
keeyeh-rehs tomahr ahlgo
Can I buy you a drink?

– Bueno, gracias.
bwehno grah-seeyahs
OK, thanks.

bottoms up

Just talking about drinks might get you intoxicated!

I want to drink tonight.
Esta noche quiero beber / tomar.
ehstah nocheh keeyeh-ro behbehr / tomahr

Let's have a drink.
Vamos a tomar un trago.
bahmos ah tomahr oon trahgo

cheers

Before you drink, make a toast.

Cheers!
¡Salud!
sahlood

A toast to your health!
¡A tu salud!
ah too sahlood

Bottoms up!
¡Fondo blanco!
fondo blahnko

hangover

Drank too much? Not feeling too well? Share your discomfort.

I have a <u>hangover</u>.

Tengo…
teh<u>ng</u>o

resaca.
reh<u>sah</u>kah

chaki. ARGENTINA
<u>chah</u>kee

goma. CENTRAL AMERICA
<u>go</u>mah
Literally: rubber

guayabo. COLOMBIA
gwah<u>yah</u>bo
Literally: guava tree

perra. ECUADOR
<u>peh</u>rrah
Literally: bitch*

caldero. PERU
kahl<u>deh</u>ro
Literally: cauldron

ratón. PERU, VENEZUELA
rah<u>ton</u>
Literally: rat

*Not that kind of bitch! This means a female dog.

7 HAVIN' FUN

beach bum

Grab your shades and get some sun.

Where's the beach?	**¿Dónde está la playa?** *dondeh ehstah lah plahyah*
Is it a nude beach?	**¿Es una playa nudista?** *ehs oonah plahyah noodeestah*
Is there a swimming pool here?	**¿Hay una piscina por aquí?** *eye oonah pees-seenah por ahkee*
Is there a lifeguard?	**¿Hay algún salvavidas?** *eye ahlgoon sahlbah-beedahs* *What you really wanna know:* *Is the lifeguard hot?!*
I want to rent …	**Quisiera alquilar …** *keeseeyeh-rah ahlkeelahr*
a deck chair.	**una silla de lona.** *oonah seeyah deh lonah*
diving equipment.	**un equipo de buceo.** *oon ehkeepo deh booseho*
a jet-ski.	**un jet-ski.** *oon yeht-skee*
a motorboat.	**una lancha de motor.** *oonah lahnchah deh motor*
an umbrella.	**una sombrilla.** *oonah sombreeyah*
a surfboard.	**una tabla de surf.** *oonah tahblah deh soorf*
water skis.	**unos esquíes acuáticos.** *oonos ehskees ahkwah-teekos*

the scoop

Cancun is a beach resort you don't wanna miss. By day, lie on the white sand beaches, take a dip in the blue waters, or go snorkeling in the sea. By night, party at any of Cancun's hot spots: Coco Bongo, DadyO, La Boom. You're guaranteed a good time when you go bar- or club-hopping along 5th Avenue; there are sports bars, trendy bars, bars right on the beach, and more.

party time

Latinos know how to have a good time.

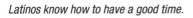

What's there to do at night?	**¿Qué se puede hacer por las noches?** *keh seh pwehdeh ahsehr por lahs nochehs*
Let's party tonight!	**¡Vamos a parrandear esta noche!** *bahmos ah pahrrahndeh-ahr ehstah nocheh*
Is there a ... in town?	**¿Hay ... en el pueblo?** *eye ... ehn ehl pwehblo*
gay club	**un club de gays** *oon kloob deh gey-ees*
nightclub	**un club nocturno** *oon kloob noktoorno*

What type of music do they play?	**¿Qué clase de música tocan?** *keh klahseh deh mooseekah tokahn*
How do I get there?	**¿Cómo se llega allí?** *komo seh yehgah ahyee*
The party was a blast!	**¡La fiesta estuvo buenísima!** *lah feeyehstah ehstoobo bwehnee-seemah*

Wanna have some fun?

– **Vamos a parrandear esta noche.**
bahmos ah pahrrahndeh-ahr ehstah nocheh
Let's party tonight.

———————————

– **Buena idea. ¿Conoces una buena discoteca?**
bwehnah eedehah. konosehs oonah bwehnah deesko-tehkah
Good idea. Do you know a good dance club?

———————————

– **¡Claro!**
klahro
Sure!

smoke

Whether you'd like to light up or want to share your distaste of smoking with those around you, here's the language you need.

| Do you mind if I smoke? | **¿Te molesta si fumo?**
teh molehstah see foomo |
| Stop smoking! | **¡Deja de fumar!**
dehkha deh foomahr |

¿Tienes un …?
teeyeh-nehs oon

cigarrillo
seegahrreeyo

faso ARGENTINA
fahso

pucho ARGENTINA, CHILE, COLOMBIA
poocho
Literally: bit

Do you have a <u>cigarette</u>?

cáncer PERU
kahnsehr
Literally: cancer

pitillo SPAIN
peeteeyo
Literally: tube

You're smoking like a chimney.

Estás fumando como una chimenea.
ehstahs foomahndo komo oonah cheemeh-nehah

spa

You need a complete detox!

I'd like …	**Quisiera …** *keeseeyeh-rah*
a facial.	**un masaje facial.** *oon mahsahkheh fahseeyahl*
a manicure.	**hacerme una manicura.** *ahsehrmeh oonah mahnee-koorah*
a massage.	**un masaje.** *oon mahsahkheh*
a pedicure.	**hacerme una pedicura.** *ahsehrmeh oonah pehdee-koorah*

I'd like …	**Quisiera …**
	kee<u>see</u>yeh-rah
a bikini wax.	**depilarme el área del bikini.**
	dehpee-<u>lahr</u>meh ehl <u>ah</u>rehah dehl
	bee<u>kee</u>nee
my eyebrows waxed.	**depilarme las cejas.**
	dehpee-<u>lahr</u>meh lahs <u>seh</u>khahs

body alterations

Blend in with the locals.

Did you have plastic surgery?	**¿Te has hecho alguna cirugía plástica?**
	teh ahs <u>eh</u>cho ahl<u>goo</u>nah seeroo<u>khee</u>ah <u>plah</u>steekah
I had …	**Me arreglé …**
	meh ahrreh<u>gleh</u>
a boob job.	**los senos.**
	los <u>seh</u>nos
a nose job.	**la nariz.**
	lah nah<u>rees</u>
a face lift.	**la cara.**
	lah <u>kah</u>rah
a tummy tuck.	**la barriga.**
	lah bah<u>rree</u>gah
I had …	**Me hice …**
	meh <u>ee</u>seh
liposuction.	**la lipo.**
	lah <u>lee</u>po
permanent make-up.	**el maquillaje permanente.**
	ehl mahkee<u>yah</u>khe pehrmah<u>nehn</u>-teh

I use botox.	**Uso botox.** _oo_so _bo_toks
He has … piercing.	**Él tiene un piercing en …** ehl _teeyeh_-neh oon _peer_seeng ehn
a belly button	**el ombligo.** ehl om_blee_go
an eyebrow	**una ceja.** _oo_nah _seh_khah
a nipple	**un pezón.** oon peh_son_
a nose	**la nariz.** lah nah_rees_
That tattoo is cool!	**¡Qué tatuaje más chévere!** keh tahtoo_ah_-keh mahs _cheh_behreh

the sights

Now that you're looking good, see and be seen.

How much does the tour cost?	**¿Cuánto cuesta el tour?** _kwahn_to _kwehs_tah ehl toor
Can we stop here …?	**¿Podemos parar aquí …?** po_deh_mos pah_rahr_ ah_kee_
to take photos	**para tomar fotos** _pah_rah to_mahr_ fotos
to buy souvenirs	**para comprar recuerdos** _pah_rah kom_prahr_ reh_kwehr_dos
to go to the bathroom	**para ir al baño** _pah_rah eer ahl _bah_nyo
Would you take a photo of us?	**¿Podría tomarnos una foto?** po_dree_-ah to_mahr_nos _oo_nah foto _Capture the memory._

73

Where's the ...?	¿Dónde está ...?
	dondeh ehstah
art gallery	**la galería de arte**
	lah gahleh-reeah deh ahrteh
botanical garden	**el jardín botánico**
	ehl khahrdeen botahneeko
castle	**el castillo**
	ehl kahsteeyo
cemetery	**el cementerio**
	ehl sehmehn-tehreeyo
church	**la iglesia**
	lah eeglehseeyah
downtown area	**el centro (de la ciudad)**
	ehl sehntro (deh lah seewdahd)
market	**el mercado**
	ehl mehrkahdo
(war) memorial	**el monumento (conmemorativo)**
	ehl monoo-mehnto (konmehmo-rahteebo)
museum	**el museo**
	ehl mooseho
nature preserve	**la reserva natural**
	lah rehsehrbah nahtoorahl
old town	**la ciudad vieja**
	lah seewdahd beeyehkhah
palace	**el palacio**
	ehl pahlahseeyo
tropical rainforest	**la selva tropical**
	lah sehlbah tropeekahl
vineyard / winery	**la viña**
	lah beenyah
What are the hours?	¿Cuáles son los horarios?
	kwahlehs son los orahreeyos

When does it close?	**¿A qué hora cierran?**
	ah keh orah seeyeh-rrahn
Can I take photos?	**¿Puedo tomar fotografías?**
	pwehdo tomahr fotograh-feeahs
How much is the entrance fee?	**¿Cuánto cuesta la entrada?**
	kwahnto kwehstah lah entrahdah
Are there any discounts for students?	**¿Hay descuentos para estudiantes?**
	eye dehskwehntos pahrah ehstoo-deeyahntehs

yo! Don't hold back—share your impressions.

It's …	**Es …**
	ehs
amazing.	**asombroso ♂ / asombrosa ♀.**
	ahsombroso / ahsombrosah
beautiful.	**hermoso ♂ / hermosa ♀.**
	ehrmoso / ehrmosah
boring.	**aburrido ♂ / aburrida ♀.**
	ahboorreedo / ahboorreedah
ugly.	**feo ♂ / fea ♀.**
	feho / fehah
Cool!	**¡Chévere!**
	chehbehreh
Super!	**¡Poderoso!** CHILE
	podehroso
Awesome!	**¡A todo dar!** MEXICO
	ah todo dahr
@#&!ing cool!	**¡De puta madre!** SPAIN
	deh pootah mahdreh
	Literally: Of a bitch mother!

75

entertainment

In the mood for a little culture?

Do you have a program of events?	**¿Tiene usted un programa de eventos?** *teeyeh-neh oostehd oon prograhmah deh ehbehntos*

Large and small towns often have guides with listings of local events; be sure to check 'em out!

Can you recommend a …?	**¿Puede recomendarme …?** *pwehdeh rehkomendahr-meh*
concert	**algún concierto** *ahlgoon konseeyehrto*
movie	**alguna película** *ahlgoonah pehleekoolah*
What time does the show start?	**¿A qué hora empieza la función?** *ah keh orah ehmpeeyeh-sah lah foonseeyon*
Where can I get tickets?	**¿Dónde puedo conseguir boletos?** *dondeh pwehdo konsehgeer bolehtos*
How much are the seats?	**¿Cuánto cuestan las entradas?** *kwahnto kwehstahn lahs ehntrahdahs*
Do you have cheaper seats?	**¿Hay entradas más baratas?** *eye ehntrahdahs mahs bahrahtahs*
What's playing at the movies?	**¿Qué películas hay en el cine?** *keh pehleekoolahs eye ehn ehl seeneh*
Is the film dubbed / subtitled?	**¿Está doblada / subtitulada la película?** *ehstah doblahdah / soobteetoo-lahdah lah pehleekoolah*

music

Get into the groove—Latino style.

I love …
: **Me encanta …**
meh ehn<u>kahn</u>tah

Latin rock.
: **el rock en español.**
ehl rok ehn ehspah<u>nyol</u>

merengue.
: **el merengue.** CARIBBEAN,
ehl meh<u>rehng</u>geh CENTRAL AMERICA

salsa.
: **la salsa.** CARIBBEAN, COLOMBIA
lah <u>sahl</u>sah

---

yo!

Can't live without your tunes? Make sure you have these.

CD player
: **reproductor de CD**
rehprodook-<u>tor</u> deh seh-<u>deh</u>

discman
: **discman**
<u>deesk</u>mahn

headphones
: **audífonos**
aw<u>dee</u>fonos

MP3 player
: **reproductor de MP3**
rehprodook-<u>tor</u> deh <u>eh</u>meh peh trehs

radio
: **radio**
<u>rah</u>deeyo

sound system
: **equipo de sonido**
eh<u>kee</u>po deh so<u>nee</u>do

SPORTS & GAMBLING

sports

Get active.

Do you like …?	**¿Te gusta …?** *teh goostah*
baseball	**el béisbol** *ehl beyeesbol*
basketball	**el básquetbol** *ehl bahskehtbol*
boxing	**el boxeo** *ehl bokseho*
cycling	**el ciclismo** *ehl seekleesmo*
skateboarding	**el monopatín** *ehl monopah-teen*
soccer	**el fútbol** *ehl footbol*

yo! Take your game to the next level.

cyclocross	**ciclocross** *seeklokros*

It's serious cycling, over rough terrain, at fast speeds.

hang-gliding	**ala delta** *ahlah dehltah*
mountain biking	**ciclomontañismo** *seeklomontah-nyeesmo*

You'll know why this is considered an extreme sport once you see the South American mountains.

rock climbing	**escalada** *ehskahlahdah*

the SCOOP

Central and South Americans are avid soccer fanatics. The most popular teams include Boca Juniors and River Plate in Argentina, América in Colombia, and Guadalajara (nicknamed Las Chivas) in Mexico. Try to catch a match at one of the huge stadiums, particularly Estadio Azteca in Mexico City. Other spectator sports include "el béisbol", baseball, in Central America; "el boxeo", boxing; and "la lucha libre", wrestling, in Mexico.

spectator sports

Prefer watching sports to actually playing them?

Is there a soccer game this Saturday?
¿Hay algún partido de fútbol este sábado?
eye ahlgoon pahrteedo deh footbol ehsteh sahbahdo

Can you get me a ticket?
¿Puede conseguirme un tiquete?
pwehdeh konseh-geermeh oon teekehteh

What's the admission charge?
¿Cuánto cuesta la entrada?
kwahnto kwehstah lah ehntrahdah

soccer match

Show that you're true sports fans—"hinchas / aficionados"—by screaming these...

Go!	**¡Hágale!** *ahgahleh*
Go for it!	**¡A ganar! / ¡Dele!** *ah gah<u>nahr</u> / <u>deh</u>leh*
Come on! / Let's go!	**¡Vamos!** *<u>bah</u>mos*
Show no mercy!	**¡Duro con ellos!** *<u>doo</u>ro kon <u>eh</u>yos* *Literally: Be rude to them!*
Beat them!	**¡Goléenlos!** *gole<u>heh</u>nlos* *Literally: Fill them with goals!*
Goal!	**¡Gol!** *gol*

score!

Share your excitement about the team's moves.

It was a/an … move! **¡Qué jugada tan …!**
keh khoogahdah tahn

magnificent **magnífica**
mahgnee-feekah

extraordinary **macanuda** ARGENTINA
mahkah-noodah

out-of-this-world **sobrada** COLOMBIA
sobrahdah

What a winner! **¡Qué golazo!**
keh golahso
Literally: Great goal!

What a game! **¡Qué partidazo!**
keh pahrtee-dahso

insults

*It's your job to harass the referee, "árbitro", humiliate the
opponent, "contrincante", and judge your team, "equipo".*

Foul! **¡Pítele!**
peetehleh
Literally: Whistle at him!

Kick him out! **¡Sáquelo!**
sahkehlo

You took a bribe! **¡Vendido!**
behndeedo
Literally: Paid for!

Damn!	**¡Malditos!** mahl<u>dee</u>tos
Your mother wears army boots!	**¡Les va la madre!**  lehs bah lah <u>mah</u>dreh *It may seem corny, but this is a pretty nasty putdown.*
Asshole!	**¡Animal!** ahnee<u>mahl</u> *Literally: Animal!*
Idiot!	**¡Bruto!** <u>broo</u>to *Literally: Stupid!*
You throw like a girl!	**¡Mucha señorita!** <u>moo</u>chah sehnyo<u>ree</u>tah *Literally: What a Miss!*
Dick!	**¡Huevón! / ¡Boludo!** ARGENTINA weh<u>bon</u> / bo<u>loo</u>do
Bastards!	**¡Cabrones!** kah<u>bro</u>nehs *Literally: Billy goats!*
Son of a bitch!	**¡Hijueputa!** eekhweh-<u>poo</u>tah

training

Don't let your body go just because you're on vacation.

| Let's … | **Vamos …** |
| | *bahmos* |

| go to the gym. | **al gimnasio.** |
| | *ahl kheemnah-seeyo* |

| exercise. | **a hacer ejercicio.** |
| | *ah ahsehr ehkhehrsee-seeyo* |

| work out with weights. | **a hacer pesas.** |
| | *ah ahsehr pehsahs* |

| work out with machines. | **a hacer máquinas.** |
| | *ah ahsehr mahkeenahs* |

ironman

Take part in Latino gym culture.

| Today I worked on the … | **Hoy hice …** |
| | *oy eeseh* |

| spinner. | **spinning.** |
| | *speeneeng* |

| stair climber. | **escaladora.** |
| | *ehskahlah-dorah* |

| treadmill. | **caminadora.** |
| | *kahmeenah-dorah* |

| Do you have … in this gym? | **¿Tienen … en este gimnasio?** |
| | *teeyeh-nehn ehn ehsteh kheemnah-seeyo* |

| a sauna | **sauna** |
| | *sawnah* |

a steam room	**baño turco**
	bahnyo toorko
massage service	**masajes**
	mahsahkhehs

gambling

Got money to burn?

Where's the racetrack?	**¿Dónde queda la pista de carreras?**
	dondeh kehdah lah peestah deh kahrrehrahs
Where can I place a bet?	**¿Dónde puedo hacer una apuesta?**
	dondeh pwehdo ahsehr oonah ahpwehstah
Is there a casino in town?	**¿Hay un casino en el pueblo?**
	eye oon kahseeno ehn ehl pwehblo
I won!	**¡Gané!**
	gahneh
I've been scammed!	**¡Me han estafado! / ¡Me tumbaron!**
	meh ahn ehstahfahdo / meh toombahron
I'm never lucky.	**Estoy salado.**
	ehstoy sahlahdo
	Literally: I'm salted.

9 MAKIN' FRIENDS

small talk

Get a conversation goin'.

My name is …	**Me llamo …** *meh yahmo* *A simple way to introduce yourself.*
What's your name?	**¿Cómo se llama?** *komo seh yahmah*
Where are you from?	**¿De dónde es usted?** *deh dondeh ehs oostehd* *Always a good ice-breaker…*
Whom are you with?	**¿Con quién viene usted?** *kon keeyehn beeyeh-neh oostehd* *Find out if he or she is single* *before things go too far.*
I'm on my own.	**Vengo solo♂ / sola♀.** *behngo solo / solah*
I'm with a friend.	**Vengo con un amigo♂ / una amiga♀.** *behngo kon oon ahmeego / oonah ahmeegah* *"Friend" is better than boyfriend* *or girlfriend, right?*
I'm with …	**Vengo con …** *behngo kon*
my boyfriend / girlfriend.	**mi novio♂ / novia♀.** *mee nobeeyo / nobeeyah*
my family.	**mi familia.** *mee fahmeeleeyah*

I'm with …	**Vengo con …**
	behngo kon
my parents.	**mis padres.**
	mees pahdrehs
my father / mother.	**mi padre♂ / madre♀.**
	mee pahdreh / mahdreh
my brother / sister.	**mi hermano♂ / hermana♀.**
	mee ehrmahno / ehrmahnah

chitchat

These will help you keep his or her attention.

What do you do?
¿Qué hace usted?
keh ahseh oostehd
_Find out some more about him
or her._

What do you study?
¿Qué estudia?
keh ehstoo-deeyah

I'm studying …	**Estudio …** *ehstoo-deeyo*
the arts.	**bellas artes.** *behyahs ahrtehs*
business.	**administración de empresas.** *ahdmeeneestrah-seeyon deh ehmprehsahs*
science.	**ciencias.** *seeyehn-seeyahs*
Whom do you work for?	**¿Para quién trabaja?** *pahrah keeyehn trahbahkhah*
I work for …	**Trabajo para …** *trahbahkho pahrah*
What are your interests / hobbies?	**¿Cuáles son sus pasatiempos?** *kwahlehs son soos pahsahteeyehmpos* *Perhaps you have something in common.*
I like …	**Me gusta …** *meh goostah*
music.	**la música.** *lah mooseekah*
reading.	**la lectura.** *lah lehktoorah*
sports.	**el deporte.** *ehl dehporteh*

Me gusta la música.

makin' plans

Get together!

Are you free for lunch?	**¿Puedo invitarle a comer / almorzar?** SPAIN *pwehdo eenbeetahrleh ah komehr / ahlmorsahr*
Can you come for a drink this evening?	**¿Puede venir a tomar una copa esta noche?** *pwehdeh behneer ah tomahr oonah kopah ehstah nocheh*
What are your plans for …?	**¿Qué planes tiene para …?** *keh plahnehs teeyeh-neh pahrah*
today	**hoy** *oy*
tonight	**esta noche** *ehstah nocheh*
tomorrow	**mañana** *mahnyahnah*
Are you free this evening?	**¿Está libre esta noche?** *ehstah leebreh ehstah nocheh*
Would you like to …?	**¿Le gustaría …?** *leh goostahreeah*
go dancing	**ir a bailar** *eer ah buylahr*
go for a drink	**ir de copas / salir a tomar algo** SPAIN *eer deh kopahs / sahleer ah tomahr ahlgo*
go for a walk	**dar un paseo** *dahr oon pahseho*
go shopping	**ir de compras** *eer deh komprahs*

Where would you like to go?	**¿Adónde le gustaría ir?** *ahdondeh leh goostahreeah eer* *Leave it up to him or her!*
I'd like to go to …	**Quisiera ir a …** *keeseeyeh-rah eer ah*
Wanna go to the movies?	**¿Vamos al cine?** *bahmos ahl seeneh*
How about another day?	**¿Qué le parece otro día?** *keh leh pahrehseh otro deeah* *Do you really mean it or are you brushing someone off?*
Thanks, but I'm busy.	**Gracias, pero estoy ocupado♂ / ocupada♀.** *grah-seeyahs pehro ehstoy okoopahdo / okoopahdah*
Can I bring a friend?	**¿Puedo llevar a un amigo♂ / una amiga♀?** *pwehdo yehbahr ah oon ameego / oonah ahmeegah*
Where should we meet?	**¿Dónde nos encontramos?** *dondeh nos ehnkontrahmos*

hangin' out

Get a little closer with these.

Let me bring you a drink.	**Voy a traerle una copa / algo de tomar.** SPAIN *boy ah trahehrleh oonah kopah / ahlgo deh tomahr*
What would you like?	**¿Qué desea?** *keh dehsehah*

| Why are you laughing? | **¿Por qué se ríe?** |
| | *por keh seh reeeh* |

Is my Spanish that bad?	**¿Es tan malo mi español?**
	ehs tahn mahlo mee ehspahnyol
	You know it's not, but it's always fun to be silly.

Wanna go somewhere quieter?	**¿Vamos a un sitio más tranquilo?**
	bahmos ah oon seeteeyo mahs trahnkeelo
	Such as...?

| Thanks for the evening. | **Gracias por la velada.** |
| | *grah-seeyahs por lah behlahdah* |

I'm afraid I have to leave.	**Lo siento, tengo que irme ahora.**
	lo seeyehn-to tehngo keh eermeh ahorah
	The evening didn't work out, huh?!

| See you soon. | **Hasta luego.** |
| | *ahstah lwehgo* |

Can I have your address?	**¿Puedo anotar su dirección?**
	pwehdo ahnotahr soo deerehk-seeyon
	Ready for a long distance relationship?

FACT Latin Americans are generally open, friendly, and helpful. But, they can be more formal than English speakers. Mind your manners when you meet someone: address someone with "señor" (Mr.), "señora" (Mrs.), "señorita" (Ms.). Also keep in mind that, in Spanish, there are three forms for you: "tú" (singular) and "vosotros" (plural, used in Spain only) are used when talking to relatives, close friends and children; "usted" (singular) and "ustedes" (plural)—often abbreviated to "Ud./Uds."— are used in all other cases. When in doubt, use "usted/ustedes".

get a date

Looking to score? Try these.

Hello, we haven't met. My name is …	**Hola, no nos conocemos. Me llamo …** *olah no nos kono**seh**mos meh **yah**mo* *Direct and to the point.*
Are you alone?	**¿Estás solo ♂ / sola ♀ ?** *eh**stahs so**lo / **so**lah* *An obvious come-on—but it's virtually foolproof.*
Why are you so lonely?	**¿Por qué tan solito ♂ / solita ♀ ?** *por keh tahn so**lee**to / so**lee**tah* *Act sweet and concerned.*
Can I buy you a drink?	**¿Quieres tomar algo?** *kee**yeh**-rehs to**mahr ahl**go* *If he or she is hot, why not?!*
Wanna dance?	**¿Bailamos?** *buy-**lah**mos* *Dancing is a popular pastime— you're certain to get a yes, "sí"!*
I'd love to have some company.	**Me encantaría tener un poco de compañía.** *meh ehnkahntah-**ree**ah teh**nehr** oon **po**ko deh kompah-**nyee**ah*
You're friendly.	**Eres simpático ♂ / simpática ♀ .** *eh**rehs** seem**pah**-teeko / seem**pah**-teeka*
You're cute.	**Eres guapo ♂ / guapa ♀ .** *eh**rehs** **gwah**po / **gwah**pah*

Too shy to approach that very attractive Latino or Latina? Try getting to know his or her friends and tell them what you think about that cutie.

That guy is …   **Ese tipo es …**
                             ehseh teepo ehs

  handsome.   **buen mozo ♂.**
                                     bwehn moso

  hot.   **un papito / papacito ♂.**
                                     oon pahpeeto / pahpahseeto
                                     Literally: a daddy

That girl is …   **Esa chica es …**
                             ehsah cheekah ehs

  attractive.   **atractiva ♀.**
                                     ahtrahk-teebah

  hot.   **una mamita / mamacita ♀.**
                                     oonah mahmeetah /
                                     mahmahseetah
                                     Literally: a mommy

She is divine.   **Ella está divina ♀.**
                             ehyah ehstah deebeenah

He's a hot guy.   **Es un tipo muy caliente ♂.**
                             ehs oon teepo mwee kahleeyehn-teh

She is good-looking.   **Tiene buena pinta ♀.**
                             teeyeh-neh bwehnah peentah

He is totally cute!   **¡Él es un tremendo bizcocho ♂!**
                             ehl ehs oon trehmehndo beeskocho
                             Literally: He is a tremen-
                             dous cupcake!

gay?

Looking for some alternative fun?

Are you gay?

¿Eres gay?
ehrehs gey

Do you like men /
women?

**¿Te gustan los hombres♂ /
las mujeres♀?**
*teh goostahn los ombrehs / lahs
mookhehrehs*

Let's go to a gay bar.

Vamos a un bar gay.
bahmos ah oon bahr gey

Do you think he's gay?

¿Será "de ambiente"?
sehrah deh ahmbeeyehn-teh
*Watch out! "De ambiente" is often
used to describe a person who is
cheerful and likes to party, no matter
what his or her sexual preferences are.*

He is gay.

Es gay.
ehs gey

She is a lesbian.

Es marimacho / maricona.
ehs mahreemahcho / mahreekonah

She plays on both teams.

Ella juega a los dos bandos.
ehyah khwehgah ah los dos bahndos

He swings both ways.

Él es de doble tracción.
ehl ehs deh dobleh trahkseeyon
*Literally: He is of double traction.
It refers to the front- and rear-
wheel drive of a car.*

FACT Buenos Aires, Argentina, is one of South America's most popular destinations for gay travelers. A progressive city, Buenos Aires recently legitimized same-sex civil unions, making this South American hotspot the first on the continent to do so. This very cool, cosmopolitan locale has a number of gay bars, clubs, saunas, etc. Try to visit during Gay Pride Parade—it's the usually the first weekend in November.

refusals

Not your type? Here are the best ways to reject someone.

No, thanks. I'm tired.	**No, gracias. Estoy cansado ♂ / cansada ♀.** *no grah-seeyahs ehstoy kahnsahdo / kahnsahda*
I am expecting someone.	**Estoy esperando a alguien.** *ehstoy ehspeh-rahndo ah ahlgeeyehn*
Don't be a pest!	**¡No moleste!** *no molehsteh*
Leave me alone!	**¡Déjeme en paz!** *dehkhemeh ehn pahs* *Literally: Leave me in peace!*
Go away!	**¡Lárguese!** *lahrgehseh*
Piss off!	**¡Písese!** COLOMBIA *peesehseh*

dating

Found a Latino lover? Here's how to describe your relationship.

We're just fooling around.	**Sólo estamos vacilando.** *solo ehstahmos bahseelahndo*
We're going out.	**Estamos saliendo.** *ehstahmos sahleeyehn-do*
We live together.	**Vivimos juntos.** *beebeemos khoontos*

affection

Ask for some lovin'.

Kiss me.	**Bésame.** *behsahmeh*
I'm feeling horny, honey.	**Estoy arrecha, cariño.** *ehstoy ahrrehchah kahreenyo*
Make love to me.	**Hazme el amor.** *ahsmeh ehl ahmor*

sex

A variety of ways to state the obvious...

We had sex.	**Tuvimos sexo.** *toobeemos sehkso*
We spent the night together.	**Pasamos la noche.** *pahsahmos lah nocheh*
We slept together.	**Dormimos juntos.** *dormeemos khoontos*

safe sex

Protection is a must, in any language.

Do you have <u>condoms</u>?

¿Tienes …?
teeyeh-nehs

condones
kondonehs

forros
forros
Literally: covers

capuchas
kahpoochahs
Literally: hoods

impermeables
eempehrmehah-blehs
Literally: raincoats

mangas
mahngahs
Literally: sleeves

Are you on the pill?

¿Tomas la píldora?
tomahs lah peeldorah

I use an IUD.

Tengo el aparato / la "T".
tehngo ehl ahpahrahto / lah teh

Should we use spermicide?

¿Usamos espuma?
oosahmos ehspoomah

Wait! I'll put in the diaphragm.

Espera, me pongo el diafragma.
ehspehrah meh pongo ehl deeahfrahgmah

STDs

Don't get caught with your pants down.

Have you been tested for STDs?

¿Te has hecho pruebas de venéreas?
teh ahs ehcho prooehbahs deh behnehrehahs

Did you get infected?

¿Te pringaron?
teh preengahron

He / She has a venereal disease.

Él ♂ / Ella ♀ tiene una enfermedad venérea.
ehl / ehyah teeyeh-neh oonah ehnfehrmeh-dahd behnehrehah

breaking up

Is that summer fling over? Say it!

Let's just be friends.

Seamos sólo amigos.
sehahmos solo ahmeegos

Let's take some time apart.

Démonos un tiempo.
dehmonos oon teeyehm-po

I'm breaking up with you.

Ya no quiero seguir contigo.
yah no keeyeh-ro sehgeer konteego

It's over between us.

Esto se acabó.
ehsto seh ahkahbo

where to shop

Grab your wallet and go!

Where's the main shopping area?	**¿Dónde está la zona principal de tiendas?** *dondeh ehstah lah sonah preensee-pahl deh teeyehn-dahs*
Where's the shopping mall?	**¿Dónde está el centro comercial?** *dondeh ehstah ehl sehntro komehr-seeyahl*
Where's …?	**¿Dónde está …?** *dondeh ehstah*
the bookstore	**la librería** *lah leebrehreeah*
the department store	**el almacén** *ehl ahlmahsehn*
the drugstore	**la farmacia** *lah fahrmah-seeyah*
the health food store	**la tienda de alimentos naturales** *lah teeyehn-dah deh ahlee-mehntos nahtoo-rahlehs*
the liquor store	**la vinetería** *lah beenehteh-reeah*
the market	**el mercado** *ehl mehrkahdo*
the music store	**la tienda de discos** *lah teeyehn-dah deh deeskos*

Where's …?	**¿Dónde está …?**
	dondeh ehstah
the newsstand	**el quiosco de periódicos y revistas**
	ehl keeosko deh pehreeyo-deekos ee rehbeestahs
the souvenir store	**la tienda de recuerdos**
	lah teeyehn-dah deh rehkwehrdos
the sports store	**la tienda de artículos deportivos**
	lah teeyehn-dah deh ahrteekoolos dehporteebos
supermarket	**el supermercado**
	ehl soopehrmehr-kahdo
When does the … open / close?	**¿A qué hora abre / cierra …?**
	ah keh orah ahbreh / seeyeh-rrah
Are you open in the evening?	**¿Abre por las noches?**
	ahbreh por lahs nochehs
Do you close for lunch?	**¿Cierran al mediodía?**
	seeyeh-rrahn ahl mehdeeyo-deeah
	Many places in Latin America break for "siesta" in the afternoon hours.

Stores throughout Latin America are generally mom n' pop shops, but large, international chain stores are starting to appear. There are also department stores in just about every large city; you'll find the latest fashions and accessories there. Smaller markets, open daily or only once a week, may carry souvenirs and clothing in addition to local produce and goods.

customer service

Need some assistance?

| Where's the … department? | **¿Dónde está la sección de …?** |
| | *dondeh ehstah lah sehkseeyon deh* |

| cosmetics | **cosméticos** |
| | *kosmehteekos* |

| shoe | **zapatos** |
| | *sahpahtos* |

| women's / men's | **damas / caballeros** |
| | *dahmahs / kahbahyehros* |

| Where's the fitting room? | **¿Dónde queda el vestier?** |
| | *dondeh kehdah ehl behsteeyehr* |

| Where can I find …? | **¿Dónde puedo encontrar …?** |
| | *dondeh pwehdo ehnkontrahr* |

| books | **libros** |
| | *leebros* |

| CDs | **CDs / Ce-des** SPAIN |
| | *seh-dehs* |

| DVDs | **DVDs / De-uve-des** SPAIN |
| | *deh-oobeh-dehs* |

| magazines | **revistas** |
| | *rehbeestahs* |

| postcards | **postales** |
| | *postahlehs* |

Looking for something in a particular color? Ask for it in…

beige	**beige** *baysh*	orange	**naranja** *nahrahn-khah*
black	**negro** *nehgro*	pink	**rosado** *rosahdo*
blue	**azul** *ahsool*	purple	**morado** *morahdo*
brown	**marrón / café** *mahrron / kahfeh*	red	**rojo** *rokho*
gray	**gris** *grees*	white	**blanco** *blahnko*
green	**verde** *behrdeh*	yellow	**amarillo** *ahmahreeyo*

sales help

Here's how to ask that cute salesperson for assistance.

Can you help me?	**¿Puede ayudarme?** *pwehdeh ahyoodahrmeh*
I'm looking for …	**Estoy buscando …** *ehstoy booskahndo*
Do you have …?	**¿Tiene usted …?** *teeyeh-neh oostehd*
I'd like to buy …	**Quisiera comprar …** *keeseeyeh-rah komprahr*

yo!

You may want to fill in those blanks with any of these items.

baseball cap	**una gorra** *oonah gorrah*
bikini	**una tanga / un bikini** *oonah tahnga / oon beekeenee*
bra	**un brasier / un sujetador** SPAIN *oon brahseeyehr / oon sookhetahdor*
(padded) bra	**un brasier con relleno** *oon brahseeyehr kon rehyehno*
bracelet	**una pulsera** *oonah poolsehrah*
briefs	**unos calzoncillos** *oonos kahlsonseeyos*
earrings	**unos aretes** *oonos ahrehtehs*
flip-flops	**chancletas** *chahnklehtahs*
halter top	**una blusa escotada** *oonah bloosah ehskotahdah*
jacket	**una chaqueta** *oonah chahkehtah*
jeans	**unos yins / unos vaqueros** SPAIN *oonos yeens / oonos bahkehros*
necklace	**un collar** *oon koyahr*
panties	**unos calzones / unas bragas** SPAIN *oonos kahlsonehs / oonahs brahgahs*
ring	**un anillo** *oon ahneeyo*

sandals	**unas sandalias**
	_oo_nahs sahn_dah_-leeyahs
skirt	**una falda**
	_oo_nah _fah_ldah
sneakers	**unos tenis**
	_oo_nos _teh_nees
sweater	**un suéter**
	oon _sweh_tehr
swimming shorts	**el pantalón de baño**
	ehl pahntah_lon_ deh _bah_nyo
swimsuit	**un vestido de baño / un bañador** SPAIN
	oon behs_teh_edo deh _bah_nyo / oon bahnyah_dor_
thong	**una tanga brasilera**
	_oo_nah _tahn_gah brahsee_leh_-rah
T-shirt	**una camiseta**
	_oo_nah kahmee-_seh_tah
watch	**un reloj de pulsera**
	oon reh_lokh_ deh pool_seh_rah

at the register

Looking to part with your hard-earned dough? Here's the lingo you need to make your purchase.

How much does it cost?	**¿Cuánto cuesta?**
	_kwahn_to _kweh_stah
Is it on sale?	**¿Tiene descuento?**
	teeyeh-neh dehs_kwehn_to

Where do I pay?	**¿Dónde se paga?** _dondeh seh pahgah_
Can I pay by credit card?	**¿Puedo pagar con tarjeta de crédito?** _pwehdo pahgahr kon tahrkhetah deh krehdeeto_
Do you accept travelers checks?	**¿Aceptan cheques de viajero?** _ahsehptahn chehkehs deh beeyah-khehro_
Could I have a receipt, please?	**¿Me podría dar un recibo, por favor?** _meh podree-ah dahr oon rehseebo por fahbor_ _Just in case you need to return something…_

bargains

Put your negotiating skills to use.

That's too expensive.	**Es demasiado caro ♂ / cara ♀.** _ehs dehmah-seeyahdo kahro / kahrah_
Is that the final price?	**¿Es ése el precio final?** _ehs ehseh ehl prehseeyo feenahl_
Do you have anything cheaper?	**¿Tiene algo más barato?** _teeyeh-neh ahlgo mahs bahrahto_
Sorry, I don't have enough money.	**Disculpe, no tengo suficiente dinero.** _deeskoolpeh no tehngo soofeeseeyehn-teh deenehro_
I'll give you 500 pesos.	**Le ofrezco 500 pesos.** _leh ofrehsko keeneeyehn-tos pehsos_
This is a real bargain!	**¡Esto es una verdadera ganga!** _ehsto ehs oonah behrdah-dehrah gahngah_

problems

Is there something wrong with your purchase?

This doesn't work.	**Esto es defectuoso.** *ehsto ehs dehfehktoo-oso*
Can you exchange this, please?	**¿Puede cambiarme esto, por favor?** *pwehdeh kahmbeeyahr-meh ehsto por fahbor*
I'd like a refund.	**Quisiera que me devolvieran el dinero.** *keeseeyeh-rah keh meh dehbolbeeyeh-rahn ehl deenehro*
Here's the receipt.	**Aquí tiene el recibo.** *ahkee teeyeh-neh ehl rehseebo*
I don't have the receipt.	**No tengo el recibo.** *no tehngo ehl rehseebo*

at the drugstore

Not feeling well? Here's some help.

| Where's the nearest pharmacy? | **¿Dónde está la farmacia más cercana?**
dondeh ehstah lah fahrmah-seeyah mahs sehrkahnah
Need one with late hours? Ask for "la farmacia de veinticuatro horas". |
| What time does the pharmacy open / close? | **¿A qué hora abre / cierra la farmacia?**
ah keh orah ahbreh / seeyeh-rrah lah fahrmah-seeyah |

Can you fill this prescription for me?	**¿Podría prepararme esta receta?** *podree-ah prehpah-rahrmeh ehstah rehsehtah*
How much should I take?	**¿Cuánto debo tomar?** *kwahnto dehbo tomahr*
How often should I take it?	**¿Cuántas veces al día debo tomarlo?** *kwahntahs behsehs ahl deeah dehbo tomahrlo*
What would you recommend for …?	**¿Qué me recomienda para …?** *keh meh rehkomeeyehn-dah pahrah*
a cold	**el resfriado** *ehl rehsfreeahdo*
a cough	**la tos** *lah tos*
diarrhea	**la diarrea** *lah deeahrreah*
a hangover	**la resaca** *lah rehsahkah*
hayfever	**la fiebre del heno** *lah feeyehbreh dehl ehno*
insect bites	**las mordeduras de insectos** *lahs mordehdoorahs deh eensehktos*
a sore throat	**el dolor de garganta** *ehl dolor deh gahrgahntah*
a sunburn	**las quemaduras de sol** *lahs kehmahdoorahs deh sol*
motion sickness	**el mareo** *ehl mahreho*
an upset stomach	**el trastorno estomacal** *ehl trahstorno ehstomahkahl*

109

Are there any side effects?	**¿Tiene efectos secundarios?** *teeyeh-neh ehfehktos sehkoondah-reeyos*
Can I get it without a prescription?	**¿Puedo conseguirlo sin receta médica?** *pwehdo konsehgeerlo seen rehsehtah mehdeekah*
Can I have …?	**¿Puede darme …?** *pwehdeh dahrmeh*
antiseptic cream	**una crema antiséptica** *oonah krehmah ahntee-sehpteekah*
aspirin	**unas aspirinas** *oonahs ahspeereenahs*
bandages	**una venda** *oonah bendah*
condoms	**unos condones** *oonos kondonehs*
insect repellent	**un repelente de insectos** *oon rehpeh-lehnteh deh eensehktos*
painkillers	**unos analgésicos** *oonos ahnahlkhehseekos*
vitamins	**unas vitaminas** *oonahs beetahmeenahs*

FACT Some pharmacies in major Spanish-speaking cities are open 24 hours; others offer a home delivery service.

For the address and phone number, consult your hotel reception or call the information line. Most pharmacies are easily recognized by their green cross and "farmacia" sign.

toiletries

aftershave
una loción para después del afeitado
oonah loseeyon pahrah dehspwehs dehl ahfey-tahdo

conditioner
el acondicionador
ehl ahkondeeseeyo-nahdor

deodorant
un desodorante
oon dehsodo-rahnteh

hairspray
la laca
lah lahkah

lipstick
el lapiz de labios
ehl lahpees deh lahbeeyos

mascara
el rimel
ehl reemehl

moisturizing cream
crema hidratante
krehmah eedrahtahnteh

razor blades
unas hojas de afeitar
oonahs okhahs deh ahfeyeetahr

sanitary napkins
unas toallas higiénicas
oonahs toahyahs eekheeyeh-neekahs

shampoo
el champú
ehl chahmpoo

soap
un jabón
oon khahbon

sunblock
el bloqueador solar
ehl blo-keh-ahdor solahr

tampons		**unos tampones** _oo_nos tahm_pon_ehs
tissues		**unos kleenex® / pañuelos de papel** _oo_nos _klee_neks / pah_ny_weh-los deh pah_pehl_
toilet paper		**un rollo de papel higiénico** oon _royo_ deh pah_pehl_ eek_heeyeh_-neeko
toothpaste		**pasta de dientes** _pahs_tah deh _deeyehn_-tehs

camera shop

Admit it, you're a tourist. You'll need these.

Where's the camera shop?	**¿Dónde está la tienda de fotografía?** _don_deh ehs_tah_ lah _teeyehn_-dah deh fotograh-_feeah_
I'm looking for a disposable camera.	**Estoy buscando una cámara desechable.** es_toy_ boos_kahn_do _oo_nah _kah_mahrah dese_chab_leh
Do you sell ... for digital cameras?	**¿Venden ... para cámaras digitales?** _behn_dehn ... _pah_rah _kah_mahrahs deekhee_tah_-lehs
memory cards	**tarjetas de memoria** tahr_khe_tahs deh meh_mo_reeyah
batteries	**baterías** bahteh_ree_ahs

I'd like this film developed, please.

Quisiera que me revelara este rollo, por favor.

kee<u>see</u>yeh-rah keh meh rehbeh<u>lah</u>rah <u>eh</u>steh <u>ro</u>yo por fah<u>bor</u>

You're old school, aren't you?!

When will the photos be ready?

Cuándo estarán listas las fotografías?

<u>kwahn</u>do ehstah<u>rahn</u> <u>lees</u>tahs lahs fotograh<u>fee</u>ahs

I'd like to pick up my photos.

Vengo a reclamar mis fotografías.

<u>behn</u>go ah rehklah<u>mahr</u> mees fotograh<u>fee</u>ahs

If you're into nature photography, then Costa Rica is where you want to be. More than 25% of this country is designated as preserved land, so an amazing amount of wildlife takes refuge here. You'll have the once-in-a-lifetime opportunity to capture the images of some 500,000 – 1,000,000 species of plants and animals. This is the photo op you've dreamed of!

internet café

Stay in touch with friends and family at home.

Is there an internet café near here?	**¿Hay algún café de internet cerca?** *eye ahlgoon kahfeh deh eentehrneht sehrkah*
Can I access the internet here?	**¿Me puedo conectar a internet aquí?** *meh pwehdo konehktahr ah eentehrneht ahkee*
What are the charges per hour?	**¿Cuánto se cobra por hora?** *kwahnto seh kobrah por orah*
Turn on the computer.	**Prende la computadora.** LATIN AMERICA *prehndeh lah kompootah-dorah*
	Enciende el ordenador. SPAIN *ehnseeyehn-deh ehl ordehnah-dor*
How do I log on?	**¿Cómo me conecto?** *komo meh konehkto*
Can I check my e-mail?	**¿Puedo revisar mi correo electrónico?** *pwehdo rehbeesahr mee korreho ehlehktroneeko* *You can also substitute "e-mail" for "correo electrónico".*
Can I download music?	**¿Puedo bajar música?** *pwehdo bahkhahr mooseekah*

yo! Where is that internet café? For info on locations, try a www search. If you're already in Spain or Latin America, find the local Tourist Information Office; it'll provide you with names, addresses, and directions for cybercafés.

computer crash

Instant IT help…

This computer doesn't respond.	**Esta computadora se quedó ahí.** *ehstah kompootah-dorah seh kehdo ahee* *Literally: This computer stayed there.*
This machine <u>froze</u>.	**Este aparato …** *ehsteh ahpahrahto* **se bloqueó.** *seh blokeho* **se congeló.** *seh konkhehlo* **se quedó colgado.** SPAIN *seh kehdo kolgahdo*

laptop

Brought your own laptop? You might need these questions.

Does this hotel / café have Wi-Fi®?	**¿Tienen en este hotel / café conexión inalámbrica a internet?** *teeyeh-nehn ehn ehsteh otehl / kahfeh konehk-seeyon eenahlahm-breekah ah eentehrneht* *In Spain, you can simply say "Wi-Fi®", which is pronounced "wee-fee".*
Where is the closest hotspot?	**¿Dónde está el punto de acceso inalámbrico más cercano?** *dohndeh ehstah ehl poontoh deh ahksehsoh eenahlahm-breeko mahs sehrkahno*

Is there a connection fee?	**¿Cobran algo por la conexión?**
	kobrahn ahlgo por lah konehk-seeyon
Do I have to register?	**¿Tengo que registrarme?**
	tehngo keh rehkhees-trahrmeh

yo! Sitting next to a cutie at a Spanish-speaking internet café or Wi-Fi® area? Spark his or her interest with these.

I love that website.	**Me encanta ese sitio.**
	meh ehnkahntah ehseh seeteeyo
	You can also use English word "website" for "sitio".
I love to chat!	**¡Me encanta chatear!**
	meh ehnkahntah chahtehahr
Give me your e-mail / (e-mail) address.	**Dame tu e-mail / tu dirección electrónica.**
	dahmeh too ee-meyeel / too deerehk-seeyon ehlehktro-neekah
Don't look at my password!	**¡No mires mi contraseña!**
	no meerehs mee kontrahsehnyah

chat room

When visiting a chat room, "canales de charla" or "salas de charla", keep in mind these abbreviations and expressions.

| How RU? | **Komotás? (¿Cómo estás?)** |
| | *No need to use opening "¿" and "¡" in a Spanish chat.* |

Where RU?	**Nonetás? (¿Dónde estás?)**
What do you want?	**Ke kieres? (¿Qué quieres?)**
	Typing "k" is faster than typing "qu"... and more fun!
Wanna go to a private chat room?	**Nos pasamos a un privado?**
	Need some alone time?!
TNX (Thanks!)	**Grax! (¡Gracias!)**
UR welcome!	**De nax! (¡De nada!)**

instant messaging

Do you require instant gratification?

phone call

From public to private, the language you need to make your call.

Can I have your phone number?	**¿Puedo anotar su número de teléfono?** *pwehdo ahnotahr soo noomehro deh tehlehfono*
Here's my number.	**Éste es mi número.** *ehsteh ehs mee noomehro*
Please call me.	**Llámeme, por favor.** *yahmehmeh por fahbor*
I'll give you a call.	**Yo lo ♂ / la ♀ llamaré.** *yo lo / lah yahmahreh*
Where's the nearest telephone booth?	**¿Dónde está el teléfono público más cercano?** *dondeh ehstah ehl tehlehfono poobleeko mahs sehrkahno*
May I use your phone?	**¿Puedo usar su teléfono?** *pwehdo oosahr soo tehlehfono*
It's an emergency.	**Es una emergencia.** *ehs oonah ehmehr-khehnseeyah*
What's the area code for …?	**¿Cuál es el código para …?** *kwahl ehs ehl kodeego pahrah*
I'd like a phone card.	**Quisiera una tarjeta de teléfono.** *keeseeyeh-rah oonah tahrkhehtah deh tehlehfono*
What's the number for Information?	**¿Cuál es el número de Información?** *kwahl ehs ehl noomehro deh eenformah-seeyon*

119

I'd like to call collect.	**Quisiera llamar por cobrar / por cobro revertido.** SPAIN
	keeseeyeh-rah yahmahr por kobrahr / por kobro rehbehrteedo
Hi. This is …	**Aló, habla …**
	ahlo ahblah
Hi?	**¿Aló?**
	ahlo
Yes?	**¿Sí?**
	see
Yes?	**¿Diga?**
	deegah
	Literally: Say?
It's me.	**Soy yo.**
	soy yo
I'd like to speak to …	**Quisiera hablar con …**
	keeseeyeh-rah ahblahr kon
Hold on.	**Un momento.**
	oon momehnto
Can you speak louder?	**¿Podría hablar más fuerte?**
	podree-ah ahblahr mahs fwehrteh
Can you speak more slowly?	**¿Podría hablar más despacio?**
	podree-ah ahblahr mahs dehspahseeyo
Would you ask him / her to call me?	**¿Podría pedirle que me llame?**
	podree-ah pehdeerleh keh meh yahmeh
Call me!	**¡Márcame!**
	mahrkahmeh
	Literally: Dial me!

hangin' up

Say good-bye with grace.

Bye.	**Adiós.** *ah<u>dee</u>yos*
Gotta go.	**Me tengo que ir.** *meh <u>tehn</u>go keh eer*
I have to hang up.	**Tengo que colgar.** *<u>tehn</u>go keh kol<u>gahr</u>*
Call me later.	**Llámame más tarde.** *<u>yah</u>mahmeh mahs <u>tahr</u>deh*
Send me a kiss before hanging up.	**Mándame un beso antes de colgar.** *<u>mahn</u>dahmeh oon <u>beh</u>so <u>ahn</u>tehs deh kol<u>gahr</u>*

text messaging

Send someone you love an SMS.

Where have you been?	**¿Dónde andas?**
Call me!	**¡Llámame!**
Kisses, Kisses	**50538 50538** *It reads "BESOS, BESOS" when you turn the wireless phone upside down.*
I love you so much.	**TQM [Te quiero mucho.]**
What do you think?	**QTPRC [¿Qué te parece?]**

Text Message	Spanish Equivalent	English Translation
¿tas aki, t pdo ver?	**¿Estás aquí, te puedo ver?**	RU here? can I CU?
no, toi okpdo	**No, estoy ocupado.**	No, I'm busy.

the SCOOP

Wireless phones are very popular in Latin America and Spain, but the service is usually very expensive, so people use them in moderation. Pre-paid plans or cards are used more frequently. In some countries, calling to a wireless phone has an extra charge for the caller, so making calls can get expensive.

In many cases, lines are blocked so only select family and friends can make a call to the phone.

FACT

Haven't used a public phone in a while, huh?! In Argentina, Colombia, Mexico, Venezuela, and Spain pick up a phone card at a newsstand. A number of Spanish-speaking countries have "locutorios", call centers, from which you can make local and international calls. To call abroad, dial 00 + country code + area code + number (country codes: Australia, 61; UK, 44; US and Canada: 1). Warning: Whether you're in Spain or Latin America, avoid making calls from your hotel room. A surcharge is almost always added and it can be hefty!

snail mail

Mail your stuff at the "Correos y Telégrafos".

Where is the nearest
post office?

¿Dónde queda la oficina de correo más cercana?
dondeh kehdah lah ofeesee-nah deh korreho mahs sehrkahnah

What time does the post
office open / close?

¿A qué hora abre / cierra el correo?
ah keh orah ahbreh / seeyeh-rrah ehl korreho

Where's the mailbox?

¿Dónde está el buzón?
dondeh ehstah ehl booson

A stamp for this postcard /
letter, please.

Una estampilla para esta postal / carta, por favor.
oonah ehstahmpeeyah pahrah ehstah postahl / kahrtah por fahbor
If you're in Spain, a stamp is "un sello".

the SCOOP

*Tired of the same ol' boring postcards? Well, in Spain, you can make your own! Spain's post office offers an online service in which you can personalize a postcard using your own photo or an image from the post office's collection. Just go to **www.correos.es** for more information.*

DICTIONARY
Spanish ➤ English

A

abono m book of subway tickets

aburrido m / **aburrida** f boring

acceso m **a Internet** Internet access

accidente m accident

acondicionador m conditioner

adicional m / f additional, extra

adiós good-bye

aeróbicos m aerobics

aeropuerto m airport

aficionado m / **aficionada** f sports fan

afuera outside

agarrar to grab, to catch

agotado m / **agotada** f worn out

agotados sold out (tickets, merchandise)

aguarapada f (Venezuela) (slang) drunk

ahogada f (Mexico) (slang) drunk

ahora now

agua m water

aire acondicionado m air conditioning

ajo m garlic

albergue m **juvenil** youth hostel

alborotos m roasted corn dessert

alimento m food

allá over there, over that way

allí there

almacén m department store

almohada f pillow

almohadilla f cushion

almuerzo m lunch

alquilar to rent

amante m / f lover

amarillo m / **amarilla** f yellow

amigo m / **amiga** f friend

analgésico m painkiller

andar to walk, to go

andén m train platform

anillo m ring

anoréxico m / **anoréxica** f anorexic

anotación f enter (on ATM)

anotar to write down

ante m coconut and almond pastry

antiséptico m / **antiséptica** f antiseptic

antro m (Mexico) (slang) dive (bar)

apagar to turn off (machine)

aparato m machine, device also IUD

apartamento m apartment

aquí here

árbitro m referee

archivo m (computer) file

arena f sand

arete m earring

arrestar to arrest

arte f art

artículos m **deportivos** sporting goods

asalto m mugging

asiento m seat

asombroso *m* / **asombrosa** *f* amazing

aspirina *f* aspirin

asqueroso *m* / **asquerosa** *f* disgusting

atletismo *m* track and field

atorar to choke

atún *m* tuna

audífonos *m* headphones

autobús *m* bus

automático *m* / **automática** *f* automatic

automovilismo *m* car racing

autoservicio self-service

autovía *f* high-speed intercity train

aventón *m* ride (hitchhiking)

ayudar to help

azul *m* / *f* blue

azúcar *m* sugar

B

bacalao *m* cod

bajar to go down, to get off (a bus, train, etc.), to download

banco *m* bank

bañador *m* (Spain) swimsuit

baño *m* bath, bathroom

bar *m* bar

barato *m* / **barata** *f* cheap

básquetbol *m* basketball

batería *f* battery

batido *m* **de leche** milkshake

beber to drink

beige *m* / *f* beige

béisbol *m* baseball

bellas artes *f* fine arts

berenjena *f* eggplant

besar to kiss

beso *m* kiss

bicicleta *f* bicycle

biela *f* (Ecuador) *(slang)* beer

bien well

billetera *f* wallet

billete *m* bill (currency) *also* (Spain) ticket

bikini *m* bikini

birra *f* (Chile, Ecuador, Bolivia, Mexico, Nicaragua, Peru) *(slang)* beer

birria *f* (El Salvador) *(slang)* beer

bizcocho *m* sponge cake

blanco *m* / **blanca** *f* white

bloqueador *m* **solar** sunblock

blusa *f* blouse

bola (El Salvador, Nicaragua) *(slang)* drunk

boleto *m* ticket

boliche *m* bowling alley *also* (Argentina) *(slang)* club

bollito *m* bread roll

bolsa *f* bag

bolso *m* purse

borracho *m* / **borracha** *f* drunk

borrar to clear (on computer, ATM)

botella *f* bottle

boxeo *m* boxing

bragas *f* (Spain) panties

brasier *m* bra

brillante *m / f* brilliant

bucear to dive

buceo *m* diving

buenísimo *m /* **buenísima** *f*
extremely good

bueno *m /* **buena** *f* good

bulímico *m /* **bulímica** *f* bulimic

butano *m* butane gas

buzón *m* mailbox

C

caballo *m* horse

café *m* coffee *also* café

caído *m* **de la perra** (Colombia)
(slang) drunk

caja *f* box

cajero *m /* **cajera** *f* cashier

cajero *m* **automático** ATM

calabaza *f* squash

caldero *m* (Peru) *(slang)* hangover

calefacción *f* heating system

caliente hot (temperature)

cama *f* bed

calzoncillos *m* briefs

calzones *m* panties

cámara *f* camera

cámara *f* **digital** digital camera

camarones *m* shrimp

cambiar to change, to exchange

cambio *m* change (money)

caminadora *f* treadmill

camión *m* (Mexico) *(slang)*
bus

camiseta *f* T-shirt

Canadá *m* Canada

canal *m* **de charla** chat room

cancelar to cancel

cáncer *m* cancer *also* (Peru)
(slang) cigarette

caña *f* sugar cane *also* a high
proof alcohol made from sugar
cane

capucha *f* hood *also (slang)*
condom

cara *f* face

carbón *m* **vegetal** charcoal

carne *f* meat

caro *m /* **cara** *f* expensive

carpa *f* tent

carro *m* car

carrito *m* **de equipaje** luggage
cart

casa *f* house

casillero *m* luggage locker

casino *m* casino

castillo *m* castle

cebolla *f* onion

ceja *f* eyebrow

cementerio *m* cemetery

cena *f* dinner

cenicero *m* ashtray

cerca de … near …

cerdo *m* pig, pork

cerradura *f* lock

cerveza *f* beer

chaki *m* (Argentina) *(slang)*
hangover

champiñón *m* mushroom

champú *m* shampoo

chancho *m* pork

chancletas *f* flip-flops

chaqueta *f* jacket

chela *f* (Mexico) *(slang)* beer

cheque *m* **de viajero** travelers check

chévere *m / f (slang)* cool

chico *m /* **chica** *f* small *also* boy / girl

choborra *f* (Peru) *(slang)* drunk

chocar to run into

chocolate *m* chocolate

chumado *m* (Ecuador) *(slang)* drunk

chupar to suck *also* (Central America, Bolivia, Peru) *(slang)* to drink

chupe *m* (Mexico) *(slang)* drink (alcoholic)

chupi *m* (Argentina) *(slang)* drink (alcoholic)

churros *m* sticks of fried, sugared dough

ciclismo *m* cycling

ciclocros *m* cyclocross

ciclomontañismo *m* mountain biking

ciego *m /* **ciega** *f* blind *also* (Spain) *(slang)* drunk

ciencias *f* science

cigarrillo *m* cigarette

cinco five

cirugía *f* surgery

cirugía *f* **plástica** plastic surgery

ciudad *f* city

clase *f* class

club *m* **de gays** gay club

club *m* **nocturno** nightclub

cocada *f* dessert made of coconut

coche *m* **cama** sleeper car (train)

cocinar to cook

colgar to hang up

collar *m* necklace

color café *m / f* brown

color *m* color

comida *m* meal, food

comida *m* **chatarra** junk food

combo *m* (Peru) *(slang)* food

¿Cómo? How?

completo *m /* **completa** *f* complete

comprar to buy

computadora *f* (Latin America) computer

con with

concierto *m* concert

condón *m* condom

conexión *f* connection

conexión *f* **inalámbrica a Internet** Wi-Fi®

confirmar to confirm

confitería *f* pastry shop

consulado *m* consulate

contrabando *m* contraband

contraseña *f* password (online)

copete *m* top of head *also* (Chile) *(slang)* drink (alcoholic)

copiosa *f* (Mexico) *(slang)* drink (alcoholic)

correo *m* mail

correo *m* **electrónico** e-mail

corrida *f* bullfight

cosa *f* thing

cosméticos *m* cosmetics

costar to cost

credencial *f* **internacional de estudiante** International Student Card

crema *f* cream

¿Cuál? Which one?

¿Cuándo? When?

¿Cuánto? How much?

cuatro four

cubata *m* (Spain) *(slang)* drink (alcoholic)

cuchara *f* spoon

cuchillo *m* knife

cuenta *f* check (in restaurant)

curado *m* / **curada** *f* (Chile) *(slang)* drunk

D

dar to give

de ida one way

de ida y vuelta round trip

dejar to leave

deletrear to spell

demasiado *m* / **demasiada** *f* too much

denunciar to report (to police)

depilar to wax (hair)

deporte *m* sports

depósito *m* deposit

desayuno *m* breakfast

descomponerse to break down

descuento *m* discount

descuidar to neglect

desear to desire, to want

desocupar to check out

desodorante *m* deodorant

despachar (Mexico) *(slang)* to eat a lot

despacio slow

despertar to wake up

detener to stop, to arrest

diabético *m* / **diabética** *f* diabetic

diafragma *m* diaphragm

diarrea *f* diarrhea

diente *m* tooth

dieta *f* diet

diez ten

dinero *m* money

dirección *f* address (street, postal)

dirección *f* **electrónica** e-mail address

disco *m* disc

discoteca *f* dance club

disfrutar to enjoy

doctor *m* doctor

documento *m* document

dólares *m* dollars

dolor *m* pain

¿Dónde? Where?

dos two

ducha *f* shower

durazno *m* peach

duro *m* / **dura** *f* hard, tough (meat)

E

efectos *m* **secundarios** side effects

él he

electrónico *m* / **electrónica** *f* electronic

ella she

ellos *m, m-f* / **ellas** *f* they

elote *m* corn

emergencia *f* emergency

encender to turn on (machine)

encontrar to find

endulzador *m* artificial sweetener

enfermedad *f* sickness, disease

enfermedad *f* **venérea** venereal disease

enfermo *m* / **enferma** *f* sick person

enlace *m* link (Web)

entrada *f* entrance fee

equipaje *m* luggage

equipo *m* sports team *also* equipment

escabiar (Dominican Republic) *(slang)* to drink

escalada *f* rock climbing

escaladora *f* stair climber

Escocia Scotland

escribir to write

España Spain

español *m* / **española** *f* Spanish

español *m* Spanish language

especial *m* / *f* special

espectacular *m* / *f* spectacular

esponja *f* sponge *also* contraceptive

esquí *m* ski

Estados Unidos, los United States

esta noche *f* tonight

estación *f* season *also* station

estampilla *f* stamp (postage)

estilo *m* style

estudiante *m* / *f* student

estudiar to study

euro *m* (Spain) local currency

excelso *m* / **excelsa** *f* sublime

exceso *m* excess

explicar to explain

exquisito *m* / **exquisita** *f* exquisite

F

falda *f* skirt

familia *f* family

fana (Argentina) *(slang)* fan (sports, music, etc.)

fanático *m* / **fanática** *f* lover (of music)

farmacia *f* drugstore

faso *m* (Argentina) *(slang)* cigarette

feo *m* / **fea** *f* ugly

fiebre *f* fever

fiebrú (Puerto Rico) *(slang)* devotee

fiesta f party

fin m end

flan m caramel custard

forro m cover *also (slang)* condom

fósforos m matches

fotografía f / **foto** photograph / photo

fresa f strawberry

fresco m / **fresca** f fresh (food)

frijoles m beans

fría f (Colombia, Guatemala, Mexico, Panama, Puerto Rico, Venezuela) *(slang)* beer

frío m / **fría** f cold, chilled

fruta f fruit

fuerte m / f strong, loud (of sounds)

fumar to smoke

funcionar to work (machine)

fútbol m soccer

G

galería f **de arte** art gallery

Gales Wales

galleta f cookie

gambas f shrimp

ganar to win

garganta f throat

garrafa f carafe

gas m gas

gaseosa f soft drink

gasolina f gasoline

gasolinera f gas station

gay gay

gerente m / f manager

gimnasio m gym

ginebra f gin

golosina f delicacy, candy

goma f gum, rubber *also* (Central America) *(slang)* hangover

gonorrea f gonorrhea

gorra f baseball cap

gracias thanks

Gran Bretaña Britain

grande m / f large

grifo m faucet

gris m / f gray

grúa f tow truck

guagua f (Caribbean) *(slang)* bus

guayaba f guava

guayabo m guava tree *also* (Colombia) *(slang)* hangover

gusano m worm

H

habitación f hotel room

hablar to talk, to speak

hacer to make, to do

hambre f hunger

hamburguesa f hamburger

heladería f ice-cream parlor

helado m ice cream

hermana f sister

hermano m brother

hermoso m / **hermosa** f beautiful

herpes m herpes

hincha m / f *(slang)* sports fan

hora hour, time
horario *m* schedule
horrendo *m* / **horrenda** *f* horrible
hotel *m* hotel
hoy today
huevo *m* egg

I

iglesia *m* church
impermeable *m* raincoat *also (slang)* condom
incendio *m* fire (in building)
información *f* information
Inglaterra England
inglés *m* / **inglesa** *f* English
inglés *m* English language
ingrediente *m* ingredient
inodoro *m* toilet
insolación *f* sunstroke
interesante *m* / *f* interesting
Internet Internet
ir de compras to go shopping
Irlanda Ireland

J

jabón *m* soap
jama *f* (Costa Rica, Cuba, Ecuador, Peru, Puerto Rico) *(slang)* food
jamón *m* ham
jardín *m* garden
jendía *f* (Puerto Rico) *(slang)* drunk
juanetazo *m* (Puerto Rico) *(slang)* drink (alcoholic)
jugo *m* juice

K

kilometraje *m* mileage

L

labio *m* lip
laca *f* hairspray
ladrón *m* thief
lancha *f* boat
langosta *f* lobster
lápiz *m* pencil
lavamanos *m* sink (bathroom)
lavandería *f* laundry
leche *f* milk
lechuga *f* lettuce
lenguado *m* sole (fish)
levantamiento *m* **de pesas** weightlifting
levantar to raise up, to lift
libra esterlina *f* British pound
librería *f* bookstore
libro *m* book
licor *m* liqueur
ligero *m* / **ligera** *f* lightweight
limón *m* lemon
limonada *f* lemonade
limpio *m* / **limpia** *f* clean
línea *f* line
linterna *f* flashlight
lipo *f* liposuction
llamada *f* telephone call
llamar to call
llave *f* key *also* faucet
llegadas *f* (on sign) arrivals
llegar to arrive

llenar to fill
llevar to take
lucha f **libre** (free-style) wrestling
lugar m place
lugar m **de moda** trendy locale
luz f light

M

madre m mother
magnífico m **/ magnífica** f magnificent
maíz m corn, maize
malo m **/ mala** f bad
mamado m (Argentina, Dominican Republic) (slang) drunk
mamar to suck also (Argentina) (slang) to drink
mamita f mommy also (slang) hottie
manga f sleeve also (slang) condom
mango m mango
manta f blanket
mantequilla f butter
manzana f apple
mañana f morning
mañana m tomorrow
mapa m map
maquillaje m make-up
maracuyá m passion fruit
mareo m motion sickness
maricona f (slang) lesbian
marimacho m (slang) lesbian
más more

masaje m massage
matraquear (Venezuela) (slang) to bribe
mecánico m mechanic
medio m **/ media** f half
melocotón m peach
menú m menu
menudo m (Mexico) beef tripe soup
mercado market
mermelada f jam, marmalade
mero m bass (fish)
mesa f table
mescal m a type of tequila
mesero m **/ mesera** f waiter / waitress
metro m subway
micro m (Chile) (slang) bus
miel f honey
mochila m backpack
molestar to bother / to annoy
moneda f coin
mono m monkey
monopatín m skateboard
monumento m memorial
morado m **/ morada** f purple
mordedura f **de insectos** insect bite
morfi m (Argentina) (slang) food
mostaza f mustard
moto f **acuática** jet-ski
motocicleta f motorbike
motocross m motocross
mucho m **/ mucha** f much, a lot

multa *f* fine, speeding ticket
museo *m* museum
música *f* music
muy very

N

nadar to swim
naranja *m / f* orange (color)
naranja *f* orange (fruit)
nariz *f* nose
natural *m / f* natural
navegar (por la Web) to surf (the Web)
negro *m / negra f* black
no no
nosotros *m / nosotras f* we
novia *f* girlfriend
novio *m* boyfriend
nueve nine
número *m* number

O

ocho eight
oficina *f* office
olvidar to forget
ombligo *m* belly button
ómnibus *m* slow and cheap train *also* (Peru) *(slang)* bus
ordenador *m* (Spain) computer
oscuro *m / oscura f* dark

P

padre *m* father
padres *m* parents
pagar to pay

pajarito *m* small bird
palacio *m* palace
panceta *f* bacon
pantalón *m* pair of pants
pantufla *f* slipper
papa *f* potato *also* (Colombia) *(slang)* food
papear (Peru, Colombia) *(slang)* to eat a lot
papel *m* paper
papel *m* **higiénico** toilet paper
papeo *m* (Spain) *(slang)* food
papelera *f* trash can
papito *m* daddy *also (slang)* hottie
paquete *m* package
para llevar to go (food)
parada *f* bus stop / subway stop
paradero *m* subway stop
parar to stop
parrandear *(slang)* to party
partido *m* game (sports match)
pasaje *m* fare, ticket price
pasaporte *m* passport
pasar to pass, to go through
pasatiempos *m* hobbies
pasillo *m* aisle
pasta *f* paste, pasta
pastel *m* cake
pastelería *f* pastry shop
patata *f* potato
patinar to skate
paz *f* peace
película *f* film, movie

pelota f ball

pensión f boarding house

pepinillo m pickle

pepino m cucumber

pequeño m **/ pequeña** f small

perdido m **/ perdida** f lost

periódico m newspaper

perra f female dog *also* (Ecuador) *(slang)* hangover

perro m dog

pescado m fish (cooked)

peso m (Argentina, Chile, Colombia, Mexico) local currency

pez m fish (live)

pezón m nipple

picante m **/** f spicy hot

píldora f pill

pimienta f pepper

piña f pineapple

piscina f swimming pool

pista f **de carreras** racetrack

pitillo m (Spain) *(slang)* cigarette

planes m plans

plata f silver

plato m plate, dish

plátano m plantain

plato m plate

playa f beach

poco m **/ poca** f not much, little

poderoso m powerful *also (slang)* super

pola f (Colombia) *(slang)* beer

policía f police

pollo m chicken

por día per day

por favor please

por hora per hour

por lo menos at least

por noche per night

por semana per week

postal f postcard

postre m dessert

(práctica f **de) ala delta** hang-gliding

precio m price

preferencia f preference, right of way

prestar to lend

primer m **/ primera** f first

próximo m **/ próxima** f next

pucho m (Argentina, Chile, Colombia) *(slang)* cigarette

pueblo m town

puerta f door, gate

pulga f flea

pulque m (Mexico) cactus beer

pulsera f bracelet

puré m **de papas** mashed potatoes

Q

¿Qué? What?

quedar to stay

quemadura f burn

¿Quién? Who?

quiosco m **de golosinas** snack bar

quiosco *m* **de periódicos y
revistas** newsstand

R

rápido fast

ratón *m* mouse *also* (Peru,
Venezuela) *(slang)* hangover

recado *m* message

receta *f* **médica** prescription

recibo *m* receipt

recuerdos *m* souvenirs

refresco *m* soft drink

regalo *m* gift

región *f* region

reiniciar to restart (computer)

reloj *m* **de pulsera** wristwatch

rendido *m* **/ rendida** *f* (Colombia)
(slang) exhausted

repelente *m* **contra insectos**
insect repellent

reproductor *m* **de CD** CD player

reproductor *m* **de MP3** MP3
player

resaca *f* hangover

reservaciones *f* reservations

reserva *f* **natural** nature preserve

resfriado *m* cold (sickness)

restaurante *m* restaurant

retiro *m* withdrawal (on ATM)

revista *f* magazine

rimel *m* mascara

robar to steal

robo *m* theft

rock *m* **clásico** classic rock

rock *m* **en español** Latin rock

rojo *m* **/ roja** *f* red

rollo *m* roll

romántico *m* **/ romántica** *f*
romantic

ron *m* rum

ropa *f* clothes

rosado *m* **/ rosada** *f* pink

rubio *m* **/ rubia** *f* blond *also*
(Bolivia) *(slang)* drunk

rugby *m* rugby

ruidoso *m* **/ ruidosa** *f* noisy

S

sal *f* salt

sala *f* **de charla** chat room

sala *f* **de espera** waiting room

salida *f* exit

salidas *f* (on sign) departures

salón *m* hall, salon

salsa *f* sauce, salsa

salmón *m* salmon

salud *f* health

salvavidas *m* lifeguard

sandalia *f* sandal

sección *f* section, department

seco *m* **/ seca** *f* dry

sed *f* thirst

seguridad *f* safety

seguro *m* insurance

seis six

selva *f* **tropical** rainforest

sencillo *m* single (hotel) room

sensacional *m* **/ f** stunning

señal *f* sign
servicio service
servilleta *f* napkin
sexo *m* sex
SIDA *m* AIDS
siesta *f* midday nap
siete seven
sífilis *f* syphilis
significar to mean
silla *f* chair
sin without
sitio *m* **Web** web site
sobornar to bribe
socado *m* **/ socao** *m* (Costa Rica) *(slang)* drunk
sol *m* sun
sombrilla *f* umbrella
sonido *m* sound
sopa *f* soup
Sudamérica South America
sudar to sweat
suéter *m* sweater
sujetador *m* (Spain) bra
supermercado *m* supermarket

T

tabla *f* **de surf** surfboard
talla *f* size (of clothing)
tampón *m* tampon
tanga *f* bikini
tanga *f* **brasilera** thong
tanque *m* tank, gas tank
tapis *m* (El Salvador) *(slang)* drink (alcoholic)

tarifa *f* price (of tickets), fare
tarjeta *f* card
tarjeta *f* **de memoria** memory card
tarjeta *f* **de teléfono** phone card
tarjeta *f* **de crédito** credit card
tasa *f* **de cambio** exchange rate
tatuaje *m* tattoo
taza *f* cup
té *m* tea
teatro *m* theater
teléfono *m* phone
televisión *f* television
televisor *m* television set
tenedor *m* fork
tener to have
tenis *m* sneakers
tequila *f* a Mexican spirit
ternera *f* veal
terrible *m* **/** *f* terrible
tienda *f* store
tienda *f* **de campaña** tent
típico *m* **/ típica** *f* typical
toalla *f* towel
toalla *f* **higiénica** sanitary napkin
tomar to take, to drink
toronja *f* grapefruit
tos *f* cough
trabajar to work (occupation)
traductor *m* **/ traductora** *f* translator
traer to bring
tragamonedas *m* slot machine
trago *m* shot (of alcohol)

trajes _m_ **de baño** swimwear
trasbocar to puke
tren _m_ train
tres three
tropical _m_ / _f_ tropical
trucha _f_ trout
tú _m_ / _f_ you (sing., inform.)
turista _m_ / _f_ tourist

U

último _m_ / **última** _f_ last
uno _m_ / **una** _f_ one
usted _m_ / _f_ you (formal)
ustedes _m_ / _f_ you (pl.) (formal, Spain)

V

vaca _f_ cow
vaqueros (Spain) cowboys _also_ jeans
vaso _m_ (drinking) glass
vegan _m_ / _f_ vegan
vegetariano _m_ / **vegetariana** _f_ vegetarian
velocidad _f_ speed
velomotor _m_ moped
venda _f_ bandage
ventana _f_ window
ventilador _m_ fan (electric)

verraquera _f_ (Colombia) _(slang)_ super
verde _m_ / _f_ green
vestido _m_ **de baño** swimsuit
vestier _m_ fitting room
viaje _m_ trip (travel)
vida _f_ life
vinatería _f_ liquor store
vino _m_ wine
viña _f_ vineyard, winery
violación _f_ rape
vitamina _f_ vitamin
vivir to live
vodka _m_ vodka
voleibol _m_ volleyball
vomitar to vomit
vuelo _m_ flight (airline)

Z

zanahoria _f_ carrot
zapallito _m_ zucchini
zapatillas _f_ (Spain) slippers
zapato _m_ shoe
zona _f_ **de campamento** campsite
zona _f_ **comercial** shopping area

DICTIONARY
English ▸ Spanish

A

to accept aceptar
access acceso *m*
accident accidente *m*
account (bank) cuenta *f*
address (e-mail) dirección *f* electrónica
address (street, postal) dirección *f*
aerobics aeróbicos *m*
AIDS SIDA *m*
airmail correo *m* aéreo
airport aeropuerto *m*
airsickness bag bolsa *f* para el mareo
aisle pasillo *m*
amazing asombroso *m* / asombrosa *f*
anorexic anoréxico *m* / anoréxica *f*
antiseptic antiséptico *m* / antiséptica *f*
apartment apartamento *m*
apple manzana *f*
arrivals (sign) llegadas *f*
to arrive llegar
artificial sweetener endulzador *m*
ashtray cenicero *m*
aspirin aspirina *f*
ATM cajero *m* (automático)

B

backpack mochila *m*
bacon panceta *f*, tocino *m*
bad malo *m* / mala *f*
bag bolsa *f*
baggage equipaje *m*
bandage venda *f*
bank banco *m*
bar bar *m*
baseball béisbol *m*
basketball básquetbol *m*
bass (fish) mero *m*
bathroom baño *m*
battery batería *f*
beach playa *f*
beans frijoles *m*
beautiful hermoso *m* / hermosa *f*
bed cama *f*
bedding ropa *f* de cama
beef carne *f* de res
beer cerveza *f*
beige beige *m* / *f*
belly button ombligo *m*
bicycle bicicleta *f*
bikini bikini *m*, tanga *f*
bill (monetary note) billete *m*
bird (small) pajarito *m*
black negro *m* / negra *f*
blanket manta *f*
blond rubio *m* / rubia *f*
blue azul *m* / *f*
book libro *m*
bookstore librería *f*

boring aburrido *m* / aburrida *f*

botanical garden jardín *m* botánico

to bother molestar

bottle botella *f*

boxing boxeo *m*

boyfriend novio *m*

bra brasier *m*, (Spain) sujetador *m*

bracelet pulsera *f*

bread pan *m*

to break down descomponerse

breakfast desayuno *m*

breasts senos *m*

briefs calzoncillos *m*

brilliant brillante *m* / *f*

to bring traer

Britain Gran Bretaña

broken roto *m* / rota *f*

brooch prendedor *m*

brother hermano *m*

brown color café *m* / *f*, marrón *m* / *f*

bulimic bulímico *m* / bulímica *f*

bullfight corrida *f*

burger hamburguesa *f*

bus autobús *m*

butter mantequilla *f*

to buy comprar

C

café café *m*

call llamada *f*

to call llamar

calorie caloría *f*

camera cámara *f*

campsite zona *f* de campamento

Canada Canadá *m*

cap (type of hat) gorra *f*

car carro *m*, (Spain) coche *m*

carafe garrafa *f*

carbonated con gas

card tarjeta *f*

car racing automovilismo *m*

carrot zanahoria *f*

cart (for luggage) carrito *m* de equipaje

casino casino *m*

castle castillo *m*

CD player reproductor *m* de CD

cemetery cementerio *m*

chair silla *f*

change (money) cambio *m*

to change cambiar

charcoal carbón *m* vegetal

chat room canal *m*, sala *f* de charla

cheap barato *m* / barata *f*

check (in restaurant) cuenta *f*

to check in presentarse

checking account cuenta *f* corriente

to check out desocupar

cheese queso *m*

chicken pollo *m*

chili pepper chile *m*

chilled frío *m* / fría *f*

chocolate chocolate *m*

to choke atorado atorar
cholesterol colesterol *m*
church iglesia *m*
cigarette cigarrillo *m*
class clase *f*
classic rock rock *m* clásico
clean limpio *m* / limpia *f*
to clear (on ATM) borrar
clothes ropa *f*
clothing store tienda *f* de ropa
club (Argentina) *(slang)* boliche *m*
cod bacalao *m*
coffee café *m*
cola coca *f*
cold frío *m* / fría *f*
cold (sickness) resfriado *m*
color color *m*
commission (fee) comisión *f*
computer (Latin America) computadora *f*, (Spain) ordenador *m*
concert concierto *m*
conditioner acondicionador *m*
condom condón *m*
confirmation number número *m* de confirmación
to confirm confirmar
consulate consulado *m*
contraband contrabando *m*
to cook cocinar
cool (temperature) fresco *m* / fresca *f*
cool *(slang)* chévere
cop policía *m* / *f*

corn elote *m*, maíz *m*
cosmetics cosméticos *m*
to cost costar
cot cama *f* plegable
cough tos *f*
cow vaca *f*
cream crema *f*
credit card tarjeta *f* de crédito
cucumber pepino *m*
cup taza *f*
currency exchange office oficina *f* / casa *f* de cambio
currency (foreign) moneda *f* extranjera
currency (local) (Argentina, Chile, Colombia, Mexico) peso *m*, (Venezuela) bolívar *m*, (Spain) euro *m*
cushion almohadilla *f*
cycling ciclismo *m*
cyclocross ciclocros *m*

D

to dance bailar
dark oscuro *m* / oscura *f*
day día *m*
decaffeinated coffee café *m* descafeinado
deck chair silla *f* de lona
delayed retrasado
delicious delicioso *m* / deliciosa *f*
deodorant desodorante *m*
department (in store) sección *f*
department store almacén *m*

departures salidas *f*

deposit depósito *m*

dessert postre *m*

diabetic diabético *m* / diabética *f*

diaphragm diafragma *m*

diarrhea diarrea *f*

diet dieta *f*

digital camera cámara *f* digital

dinner cena *f*

discount descuento *m*

disease enfermedad *f*

disgusting asqueroso *m* / asquerosa *f*

dish plato *m*

to dive bucear

dive (bar) (Mexico) *(slang)* antro *m*

doctor doctor *m*

document documento *m*

dollars dólares *m*

door puerta *f*

to download bajar

downtown (area) centro *m* de la ciudad

draft (beer) cerveza de barril *m*

to drink beber, tomar

drink bebida *f*

to drip gotear

to drive manejar, conducir

drugstore farmacia *f*

drunk borracho *m* / borracha *f*

E

earring arete *m*

to eat comer

egg huevo *m*

eggplant berenjena *f*

eight ocho

e-mail correo *m* electrónico

emergency emergencia *f*

England Inglaterra

English inglés *m* / inglesa *f* (person) *also* inglés *m* (language)

to enjoy disfrutar

enough suficiente *m* / *f*

entrance fee entrada *f*

equipment equipo *m*

espresso café *m* exprés

exchange rate tasa *f* de cambio

to exchange cambiar

to exercise hacer ejercicio *m*

exit salida *f*

expensive caro *m* / cara *f*

to explain explicar

exquisite exquisito *m* / exquisita *f*

extra adicional

eyebrow ceja *f*

F

face cara *f*

facial masaje *m* facial

family familia *f*

fan (electric) ventilador *m*

fare tarifa *f*, pasaje *m*

fast rápido

fast food comida *f* rápida

father padre *m*

faucet llave *f*

fever fiebre *f*

file (computer) archivo *m*
to fill llenar
first primer *m* / primera *f*
fish (cooked) pescado *m*
fish (live) pez *m*
fitting room vestier *m*, probador *m*
five cinco
flashlight linterna *f*
flea pulga *f*
flight vuelo *m*
flip-flops chancletas *f*
food alimento *m*, comida *f*
foreign currency moneda *f* extranjera
to forget olvidar
fork tenedor *m*
four cuatro
fresh fresco *m* / fresca *f*
fried frito *m* / frita *f*
friend amigo *m* / amiga *f*
fries papas *f* fritas, papas a la francesa
fruit fruta *f*

G

gallery galería *f*
game (sports match) partido *m*
garden jardín *m*
garlic ajo *m*
gas gas *m*
gas station gasolinera *f*, estación *f* de gasolina
gas tank tanque *m*
gasoline gasolina *f*

gay gay
to get off (a bus, train, etc.) bajar
gift shop tienda *f* de regalos
gin ginebra *f*
girlfriend novia *f*
to give dar
glass (drinking) vaso *m*
gluten-free sin gluten
gonorrhea gonorrea *f*
good bueno *m* / buena *f*
grapefruit toronja *f*
gray gris *m* / *f*
green verde *m* / *f*
guava guayaba *f*
guest huésped *m* / huéspeda *f*
guesthouse casa *f* de huéspedes
gym gimnasio *m*

H

hairspray laca *f*
halter top blusa *f* escotada
ham jamón *m*
hamburger hamburguesa *f*
to hang up colgar
hang-gliding (práctica *f* de) ala delta
hangover resaca *f* *also* (Argentina) *(slang)* chaki *m*, (Central America) *(slang)* goma *f*, (Colombia) *(slang)* guayabo *m*, (Ecuador) *(slang)* perra *f*, (Peru) *(slang)* caldero *m*, (Peru, Venezuela) *(slang)* ratón *m*
to have tener
hay fever fiebre *f* del heno

he él
headphones audífonos *m*
health salud *f*
health food store tienda *f* de alimentos naturales
heating system calefacción *f*
hello hola
to help ayudar
here aquí
herpes herpes *m*
hobbies pasatiempos *m*
horrible horrendo *m* / horrenda *f*
horse caballo *m*
hot (temperature) caliente *also* **(spicy)** picante
hotel hotel *m*
hottie *(slang)* mamita *f* / papito *m*
hour hora *f*
house casa *f*
How? ¿Cómo?
to be hungry tener hambre

I

ice hielo *m*
ice cream helado *m*
ice-cream parlor heladería *f*
information información *f*
ingredient ingrediente *m*
insect insecto *m*
insurance seguro *m*
interesting interesante *m* / *f*
International Student Card credencial *f* internacional de estudiante

Internet access acceso *m* a Internet
Internet café café *m* Internet
Ireland Irlanda
itemized bill factura *f* detallada
IUD aparato *m*, la "T" *f*

J

jacket chaqueta *f*
jai alai pelota *f* vasca
jam mermelada *f*
jeans jeans *m*, (Spain) vaqueros *m*
jet-ski moto *f* acuática
juice jugo *m*
junk food comida chatarra *f*

K

key llave *f*
kiss beso *m*
to kiss besar
knife cuchillo *m*

L

large grande *m* / *f*
last último *m* / última *f*
later más tarde
Latin rock rock *m* en español
laundry service servicio *m* de lavandería
to leave dejar
lemon limón *m*
lemonade limonada *f*
to lend prestar
lesbian *(slang)* marimacho *m* / maricona *f*

lettuce lechuga *f*
life vida *f*
lifeguard salvavidas *m*
to lift levantar
light luz *f*
link (Web) enlace *m*
lip labio *m*
liposuction lipo *f*
lipstick lápiz *m* de labios
liqueur licor *m*
liquor store vinatería *f*
list lista *f*
to live vivir
lobster langosta *f*
lock cerradura *f*
locker casillero *m*, lócker *m*
lost perdido *m* / perdida *f*
lost and found oficina *f* de objetos perdidos
loud fuerte *m* / *f*
lover amante *m* / *f*
low-calorie bajo en calorías *f*
low-cholesterol bajo en colesterol *m*
low-fat bajo en grasa *f*
low-sodium bajo en sodio *m*
luggage equipaje *m*
lunch almuerzo *m*

M

magazine revista *f*
magnificent magnífico *m* / magnífica *f*
mailbox buzón *m*

make-up maquillaje *m*
manager gerente *m*
map mapa *m*
market mercado *m*
marmalade mermelada *f*
mascara rimel *m*
massage masaje *m*
matches fósforos *m*
meal comida *f*
meat carne *f*
mechanic mecánico *m*
memorial monumento *m*
memory card tarjeta *f* de memoria
menu menú *m*
message recado *m*
mileage kilometraje *m*
milk leche *f*
milkshake batido *m* de leche
mineral water agua *m* mineral
mini-bar mini-bar *m*
mistake error *m*
moisturizing cream crema *f* humectante
money dinero *m*
moped velomotor *m*
morning mañana *f*
mother madre *m*
motion sickness mareo *m*
motocross motocross *m*
motorbike motocicleta *f*
motorboat lancha *f* de motor
mountain biking ciclomontañismo *m*

movie película *f*

movie theater cine *m* múltiple

MP3 player reproductor *m* de MP3

much mucho *m* / mucha *f*

mugging asalto *m*

museum museo *m*

mushroom champiñón *m*

music música *f*

mustard mostaza *f*

my mi *m* / *f*

N

nap (midday) siesta *f*

napkin servilleta *f*

nature preserve reserva *f* natural

near ... cerca de ...

nearby por aquí

nearest más cercano *m* / cercana *f*

necklace collar *m*

newsstand quiosco *m* de periódicos y revistas

next próximo *m* / próxima *f*

night noche *f*

nightclub club *m* nocturno

nine nueve

nipple pezón *m*

no no

noisy ruidoso *m* / ruidosa *f*

non-carbonated sin gas

non-smoking area sección *f* de no fumadores

nonstop bus autobús *m* sin escalas

nose nariz *f*

now ahora

nude beach playa *f* nudista

number número *m*

O

office oficina *f*

old town ciudad *f* vieja

on time a tiempo

one uno *m* / una *f*

one-way de ida

onion cebolla *f*

orange (color) naranja *m* / *f* also **(fruit)** naranja *f*

order pedir

outside afuera

P

package paquete *m*

pain dolor *m*

painkiller analgésico *m*

palace palacio *m*

panties calzones *m*, (Spain) bragas *f*

paper papel *m*

parents padres *m*

party fiesta *f*

to party *(slang)* parrandear

passport pasaporte *m*

password (online) contraseña *f*

pastry shop pastelería *f*, confitería *f*

to pay pagar

pay phone cabina *f* telefónica

peach durazno *m*, melocotón *m*

pencil lápiz *m*

per day por día

per hour por hora

per night por noche

per week por semana

phone teléfono *m*

photograph fotografía *f*

pickle pepinillo *m*

pig cerdo *m*

pill píldora *f*

pillow almohada *f*

pineapple piña *f*

pink rosado *m* / rosada *f*

plans planes *m*

plantain plátano *m*

plastic surgery cirugía *f* plástica

plate plato *m*

platform (train station) andén *m*

please por favor

police policía *f*

pool piscina *f*

pop music música *f* pop

pork cerdo *m*, chancho *m*

post office oficina *f* de correo

postage tarifa *f* de correo

postcard postal *f*

potato papa *f*, patata *f*

pounds (British) libras esterlinas *f*

prescription receta *f* médica

price precio *m*

program of events programa *m* de eventos

to puke trasbocar

purple morado *m* / morada *f*

purse bolso *m*

R

racetrack pista *f* de carreras

rainforest selva *f* tropical

to raise up levantar

rape violación *f*

rat ratón *m*

razor blade hoja *f* de afeitar

receipt recibo *m*

to recommend recomendar

red rojo *m* / roja *f*

red wine vino *m* tinto

referee árbitro *m*

rent alquilar

to repeat repetir

to report (to police) denunciar

reservation reservación *f*

to reserve reservar

restart (computer) reiniciar

restaurant restaurante *m*

rice arroz *m*

ride (hitchhiking) aventón *m*, viaje *m*

ring anillo *m*

rock climbing escalada *f*

rock (music) música *f* rock

roll (of bread) bollito *m*

roll (of toilet paper) rollo *m* de papel higiénico

romantic romántico *m* / romántica *f*

room (hotel) habitación f de hotel

room service servicio m de habitación

round trip de ida y vuelta

rugby rugby m

rum ron m

to run into chocar

S

safe (box) caja f fuerte, caja f de seguridad

safety seguridad f

salmon salmón m

salt sal f

sand arena f

sandal sandalia f

sanitary napkin toalla f higiénica

satellite TV televisión f satélite

savings account cuenta f de ahorros

schedule horario m

science ciencias f

scrambled eggs huevos m revueltos

seat asiento m

security check seguridad f

service servicio m

set menu menú m del día

seven siete

sex sexo m

shampoo champú m

she ella

shoe zapato m

shop tienda f

shopping area zona f comercial

to go shopping ir de compras

shower ducha f

shrimp gambas f, camarones m

sick enfermo m / enferma f

sickness enfermedad f

side effects efectos m secundarios

single (hotel) room sencillo m, habitación f sencilla

sink (bathroom) lavamanos m

sister hermana f

six seis

size (of clothing) talla f

skateboard monopatín m

ski esquí m

skirt falda f

sleeper car coche m cama

sleeping bag saco m de dormir

slippers pantuflas f, (Spain) zapatillas

slot machine tragamonedas m

small pequeño m / pequeña f

to smoke fumar

smoking area sección f de fumadores

snack bar cafetería f, quiosco m de golosinas

sneakers tenis m

soap jabón m

soccer fútbol m

sodium sodio m

soft drink gaseosa f, refresco m

sole (fish) lenguado *m*

sore throat dolor *m* de garganta

so-so regular

sound system equipo *m* de sonido

soup sopa *f*

South America Sudamérica

souvenirs recuerdos *m*

Spain España

Spanish (person) español *m* / española *f* also **(language)** español *m*

to speak hablar

speakers parlantes *m*

special especial *m* / *f*

spectacular espectacular *m* / *f*

to spell deletrear

sponge esponja *f*

spoon cuchara *f*

sports deporte *m*

sports fan *(slang)* hincha *m* / *f*, aficionado *m* / aficionada *f*

sports store tienda *f* de artículos deportivos

sportswear ropa *f* deportiva

squash calabaza *f*

stair climber escaladora *f*

stamp (postage) estampilla *f*

star fruit carambola *m*

station estación *f*

to stay quedar

to steal robar

steam room baño *m* turco

to stop parar

store tienda *f*

strawberry fresa *f*

student estudiante *m* / *f*

to study estudiar

stunning sensacional *m* / *f*

style estilo *m*

sublime excelso *m* / excelsa *f*

subway metro *m*

succulent suculento *m* / suculenta *f*

sugar azúcar *m*

suitcase maleta *f*

sun sol *m*

sunblock bloqueador *m* solar

sunburn quemadura *f* de sol

sunstroke insolación *f*

super (Chile) poderoso *m*, (Colombia) la verraquera *f*

supermarket supermercado *m*

surf the Web navegar por la Web

surfboard tabla *f* de surf

to swallow tragar

to sweat sudar

sweater suéter *m*

sweet dulce *m* / *f*

sweetener (artificial) endulzador *m*

to swim nadar

swimming pool piscina *f*

swimming trunks pantalón *m* de baño

swimsuit vestido *m* de baño, (Spain) bañador *m*

swordfish pez *m* espada

syphilis sífilis *f*

T

table mesa *f*
to take tomar, llevar
tampon tampón *m*
tank tanque *m*
tattoo tatuaje *m*
taxi taxi *m*
tea té *m*
telephone teléfono *m*
television televisión *f*
ten diez
tent tienda *f* de campaña *f*
terrible terrible *m* / *f*
thanks gracias
theater teatro *m*
theft robo *m*
they ellos *m*, *m-f* / ellas *f*
there allí
thief ladrón *m*
thing cosa *f*
to be thirsty tener sed *f*
thong tanga *f* brasilera
three tres
throat garganta *f*
ticket (Latin America) boleto *m*, (Spain) billete *m*
tip (for service) propina *f*
tire llanta *f*
toast pan *m* tostado
today hoy
to go (food) para llevar
toilet inodoro *m*

tomorrow mañana *m*
tonic water agua *m* tónica , agua *m* quina
tonight esta noche *f*
tooth diente *m*
toothpaste pasta *f* de dientes
tourist turista *m* / *f*
tow truck grúa *f*
towel toalla *f*
town pueblo *m*
track and field atletismo *m*
train tren *m*
to translate traducir
translator traductor *m* / traductora *f*
trash can papelera *f*
travelers check cheque *m* de viajero
treadmill caminadora *f*
trip (travel) viaje *m*
trout trucha *f*
T-shirt camiseta *f*
tuna atún *m*
turkey pavo *m*
to turn off (machine) apagar
to turn on (machine) encender
two dos

U

ugly feo *m* / fea *f*
umbrella sombrilla *f* / paraguas *m*
to understand entender
United States los Estados Unidos

V

vanilla vainilla *f*

veal ternera *f*

vegan vegan *m* / *f*

vegetable soup sopa *f* de verduras

vegetarian vegetariano *m* / vegetariana *f*

venereal disease enfermedad *f* venérea

vinaigrette salsa *f* vinagreta

vineyard viña *f*

vitamin vitamina *f*

vodka vodka *m*

volleyball voleibol *m*

to vomit vomitar

W

waiter / waitress mesero *m* / mesera *f*

waiting room sala *f* de espera

to wake up despertar

wallet billetera *f*

water agua *m*

to wax (hair) depilar

we nosotros *m*, *m-f* / nosotras *f*

web page página *f* Web

web site sitio *m* Web

week semana *f*

weekend fin *m* de semana

weightlifting levantamiento *m* de pesas

What? ¿Qué?

When? ¿Cuándo? *also* ¿A qué hora …?

Where? ¿Dónde?

white blanco *m* / blanca *f*

Who? ¿Quién?

Wi-Fi® conexión *f* inalámbrica a Internet

to win ganar

window ventana *f*

wine vino *m*

winery viña *f*

with con

to withdraw retirar

withdrawal (of money) retiro *m*

without sin

to work (machine) funcionar

to work (occupation) trabajar

worm gusano *m*

wrestling (free-style) lucha *f* libre

wristwatch reloj *m* de pulsera

to write escribir

to write down anotar

Y

yellow amarillo *m* / amarilla *f*

yes sí

you tú *m* / *f* (sing., informal), usted *m* / *f* (sing., formal), ustedes *m* / *f* (pl.)

youth hostel albergue *m* juvenil

Z

zucchini zapallito *m*